Presented to

_____

by

_____

on the occasion of

_____

Date

_____

# Feeding in
# His Pasture

Inspiring poems to grow in Christ

**Audrey Hill**

# Feeding in His Pasture

## Inspiring poems to grow in Christ

**Author**
Audrey Hill

**Editor**
J. Alan Mostert

**Literary consultant**
Tibo Mlik

**Cover photo**
Shah Tahsin Anwar

**Design and layout**
Nicky Wenhold

Hardback ISBN 978-1-967667-00-0
Paperback ISBN: 978-1-967667-01-7
E-Book ISBN: 978-1-967667-02-4

First edition 2025
Melbourne, Florida
Copyright © 2025 by Inkpot, LLC
Publisher: Inkpot, LLC

My sheep hear my voice, and I know them,
and they follow me: and I give unto them eternal life;
and they shall never perish, neither shall any man
pluck them out of my hand.

*John 10:27, 28 (KJV)*

This book is dedicated
to my loving family:
my godly, faithful, husband Ron
and our daughter Ronda,
who are in heaven,
waiting for Nathan, our special needs son,
and me, to join them
someday.

# Contents

# Foreword

*Feeding in His Pasture* is a collection of inspirational poems and prayers by Audrey Hill. Throughout her life, Audrey Hill has written these edifying, biblical and godly writings, honoring the Lord Jesus Christ. *Feeding in His Pasture* is a book to be used in personal devotions and reflections, of the God of all creation. A new believer in Christ enjoys *Feeding in His Pasture*, as well as any individual who is mature in the Lord. It is a blessing to read!

Audrey Hill has been my aunt, on my mother's side of the family, for over 60 years. Living in the south suburbs of Chicago, Illinois, it was always a special time going out to Uncle Ron and Aunt Audrey's farm. Memorial Day and Labor Day family gatherings throughout the younger years of my life, made great memories for me. Being an adopted child, and with my uncle and aunt not having any children of their own at that time, they always seemed to give me a little extra attention. It was something that I will always cherish, deep down in my heart. They later adopted a daughter and son.

As with some families, when everyone grows older, there are drifting periods, when I would only see my uncle and aunt, either when there was a family wedding or a funeral of someone in the family.

Sadly, in August of 2014, my cousin Ronda, my uncle and aunt's daughter, tragically passed away in her sleep while she was on vacation, visiting relatives and a friend, on Long Island, New York. That hit my uncle and aunt hard. Their unwavering faith in the Lord carried them through that very hard time in their lives.

My Uncle Ron began to start having health issues. My aunt became his caregiver until his passing in 2019. After my uncle passed away, I knew that my aunt was alone. That was when the Lord started tugging at my heart, to contact her and see how she was doing.

I am so glad that I reached out to her. It has been a wonderful thing for both of us; it was not a coincidence that I made that call. We have been able to share our faith, walk together by talking about the scriptures, singing old hymns, praying and watching YouTube. We would have great fellowship together, with an occasional breakfast or lunch as well.

Over the years, at Christmas, my aunt would send out a poem, with a Christmas theme and let us know how her family was doing. I always enjoyed reading her letters.

After spending more and more time with my aunt, I came to find out that she is a prolific writer of many, many poems and prayers. Because she has been homebound and cannot get around like she once did, that did not deter her from sharing the gospel. She accomplished this through telephone conversations with anybody that she came in contact with and also through her Facebook page. The idea of publishing her writings came about after many conversations. Starting in the fall of 2022, where on many occasions, my aunt was led to tears about heaven and hell and about wanting to see souls won for the kingdom of God. When she said that, immediately my eyes focused in on the numerous books of poems and prayer writings that she had on a book shelf, in her living room. I said "Aunt, there is where your legacy for the kingdom is, right there," and I pointed out to her the books of writings that she penned over many decades. They were sitting on a shelf, collecting dust. I told her that the world needed to hear those writings because they will make a difference for eternity. After much thought and prayer, she gave me the approval to publish her writings. This was the beginning of *Feeding in His Pasture*.

I called an old friend of mine, named Alan Mostert. Growing up together, we took part in sports and church activities. We were involved in many church young adult basketball games and church camps, in the summers and winters, during our teenage years.

The Lord radically changed Alan's heart and led him to the mission field. He went to the country of Grenada, West Indies, in the Caribbean Sea. On August 6, 1976, Alan's life, suddenly and stunningly took a different path, after he broke his neck in a diving accident. It happened while he was preparing for a children's church camp, along the Caribbean shore. Even though he became paralyzed, he is still living his life for the Lord Jesus Christ. Alan wrote about his accident in the book *Grown Ups From Pacesetter* by Scott W. Wesley. The chapter titled, "Final Dive on a Caribbean Island," is the story of Alan's accident.

After Alan returned back home to the United States, the Lord brought him preaching and teaching opportunities. I truly and genuinely have seen his faith never waver throughout this journey. I admire him immensely and I tell his amazing story whenever I'm led or asked to do so.

After Alan retired as a securities broker, he began publishing books. During our telephone conversation, I asked him how he was, and what he was doing. When he told me that he was publishing books, I told him that I was looking for a publisher for my aunt's poems. I said to him that this is not a coincidence, that after many, many years the Lord led me to contact him to get these writings published for my aunt. What an amazing God!

*Feeding in His Pasture* is a powerful tool for pastors, teachers, and any other individual related to the instruction of the Bible. *Feeding in His Pasture* contains categories of scripture for every occasion. Evangelism, eternity, worship, Christmas and many more topics can easily and quickly located to be read and enjoyed, by one person or group. Every child of God should own a copy of *Feeding in His Pasture* for their sessions of praise and worship of glorifying God.

It is my genuine hope and prayer that *Feeding in His Pasture* will bless you mightily, to not only know who Jesus is and to make Him your savior, but also, to grow in the grace and the knowledge of our Lord Jesus Christ.

*Allen Slager, Sr.*

# Preface

First and foremost, I am so very, very thankful that I was born and raised in a Christian home. Henry and Alice Muys, my parents, created a godly atmosphere, in our home. Always guiding us in the truths of Christ, they taught my three older siblings and me, Christian values. My oldest sister, Eleanor, was 16 years older than me. My brother, Bill, was 14 years older and Shirley, was nine years older than me.

Our family lived in Roseland, on the south side of Chicago, Illinois. I played with the kids in the neighborhood. We would put skates on over our shoes and skate up and down the smooth street. We dressed up in old lace curtains and played wedding. We played hop scotch, hide and seek and other games, until the street lights came on. We had Kool-Aid stands and roasted potatoes in the back prairie, by the railroad tracks. Sometimes, the train engineer would throw out big pieces of chalk that we would use to draw on our street.

My father read his Bible regularly and prayed faithfully. As a child, I'd rush noisily into the back door and my mother would tell me to, "Shhh," and say, "Daddy is praying." I would tip toe to the bedroom and see my father on his knees.

One night when I was a child my daddy said to me, "Come, let's go outside. There is something you must see." Together, we stood in the yard, and he said, "Look at the sky. Look and see the heavens."

I said, "OK, but why?"

"God made all those twinkling stars. There are many you can't see. He's the God of creation and He made both you and me." Something was instilled in me. A sweetness filled the air. I sensed the awesomeness of God as we stood together there.

When I was sick in bed, my daddy would come in and tell me a Bible story. Over and over, I always wanted to hear about Noah and the ark. Dad witnessed to a lot of people, and led many people to the Lord.

One evening, when I was nine years old, I was sent to bed for misbehaving. In the darkness of my bedroom, I started thinking that I was not saved. I started feeling very bad for how I had acted, which was the Holy Spirit convicting me. I began to cry and thought, "What if Jesus would come back, or what if I died?" I would be left behind, as my parents would go to heaven. Even worse, I would go to Hell if I died! Thinking, if I went to sleep, I wouldn't feel so bad but my guilty conscience kept me awake. It seemed like the more I tried to fall asleep, the harder it became. I knew I was a sinner and wanted forgiveness of my sins. I was wondering if I should call down to my parents, since I had been so bad earlier. I had to get saved! So, I called down to them. My father came to my room. I told him I wanted to get saved, by asking Jesus into my heart. When my dad saw my tearful eyes and heard my quivering voice, he knew I was serious. He led me downstairs to the living room. Together, kneeling by the couch, my father led me to the Lord. Praying a simple prayer, I gave my life to Jesus, who died for all my sins. Right there in our living room, on a cold winter night, Jesus saved me. Relieved, knowing I was safe in my new savior Jesus Christ; I would live forever with Him. As I wiped away my tears, I saw the window panes on our house. They were *frosty white*. The poem, "Frosty White," which is in the category, *Salvation*, in *Feeding in His Pasture*, talks about that night.

I had a wonderful mother. She sewed a lot of my clothes, especially for special occasions. While I was in grammar school, I vividly remember one very cold day, around Christmas. My mother walked several blocks to my school, to attend our program. As my class was getting ready to sing, I looked up in the balcony, to try to find my mother. Yes! There she was, waving to me with her white gloves.

On Saturday night, she would put rags in my hair so I would have curls on Sunday. While braiding my hair, I would face the south wall in the kitchen, and saw a plaque that read, "Only one life, twill soon be past, only what's done for Christ will last." I have no idea how many times I read that plaque but it was definitely instilled in me. *Rags* were worn out sheets cut into strips. Bill used to tease me about this. He'd come home on Saturday night, after I had gone to sleep. The next day he'd say to me, "All I saw were white "*things*," sticking up in your bed, last night." Ha!

Every weekend my mother would bake raisin and white bread. I couldn't wait for the raisin bread to cool, and have a slice with butter. If we were having company after church on Sunday night, she would bake a cake. On Friday after school, I would walk with my mother, in all kinds of weather, to the "Ave," where we would shop. We'd go to Gately's Peoples Store. I'd help her carry groceries home.

My parents listened to the real-life radio program "Unshackled," on Saturday evenings. "Unshackled," is the last live radio drama broadcast in the nation. The name comes from stories of people who have given their life to Christ, and thereby become unshackled, by sin. It is produced by Pacific Garden Mission, in Chicago, Illinois. My parents were both of Dutch descent and would often speak in Dutch. I would ask, "What does that mean in English?" Most of the time, my mother could not think of a word in English that would mean the same thing.

As a family, after supper we would always read the Bible. Eleanor would read out loud. Sometimes, she could not pronounce the names in the Old Testament and my mother would say, "That's enough."

We never had a car. We walked to the meetings at the assemblies, three times every Sunday; summer, fall, winter and spring. On Sunday morning, we gathered to remember the death of the Lord Jesus Christ. We sat around a small table, covered with a snow white tablecloth, with a loaf of bread and a goblet of wine, in the middle. The women all wore head coverings and the men would lead in different types of worship, as God led them. They would give out a hymn, pray or share a portion of scripture. An elder would thank the Lord for his broken body. Then, the bread, representing Christ's body, was passed from one person to another. A second elder would thank the Lord for the wine, representing the Lord's blood. The goblet of wine was then passed from one person to another.

After the meeting ended, we walked home, ate dinner and I'd walk back for Sunday school, which started at 2 p.m. At 7 p.m. we walked back for the gospel meeting. I very well remember the night meetings! We would sit up near the front because my mother was hard of hearing. Most of the time, a man by the name of Andy Hoekstra, would lead the singing. I loved it when he would preach. He sang at Eleanor and Ted's wedding.

During the winter, we had children's meetings on Friday night. One night, as my father and I were walking home, it was bitter cold. As we walked under the street light, I could see my dad's breath and his nose dripping. He told me to close my mouth and breathe through my nose because the cold air was hard on my lungs.

I was six years old when Eleanor got married. My mother wrote a song for me to sing at her wedding. She chose the melody of, "Sweet Hour of Prayer." After I sang it, they made me stand up on a chair and sing it again.

"This day we've long been waiting for
God bless you Ted and Eleanor
And may He keep you day by day
While you're at work and I'm at play.
We all miss your friendly smile
So please drop in and stay for a while,
We'll miss you Eleanor and Ted
But thanks for giving me your bed."

Shirley, was my mentor and I loved her hand-me-downs. She had very handsome boyfriends. I was her maid of honor when she got married. I well remember the day Shirley bought a T.V. I think we were the last ones on the block to get one.

My dad was not well. As his sickness progressed, he had to stop doing things for the Lord. When I was about six years old, I was in the nearby drug store. There were a few boys in there, who were in my father's Sunday school class. I told them that he wouldn't be able to teach the class anymore. I still remember their reactions. They moaned and said, "Oh no! He was the best teacher we ever had!" He had hardening of the arteries, which affected his brain and he did not know who we were the last few years of his life.

I graduated from Brennan Grammar School. After school, I would hurry home, to either draw, color and/or paint. I received an art scholarship from the Art Institute of Chicago when I was in high school, but could not use it. I had to find a job. My parents, Shirley and I moved upstairs from Eleanor, Ted and their daughter, Sandy. I graduated from grammar school and that summer my father passed away. He died July, 1955. I was 14 and had just graduated from grammar school. Shirley married John Slager Jr., so it was just my mother and me.

In high school I was in a large young people's choir. A few friends and I would travel up to Chicago on Saturday mornings to practice. We sang in different places. One summer we went to Estes Park, Colorado on the train for a big Christian young people's convention. Little did I know that my mother was seriously ill. In fact, the doctor had said that she had a blood clot and she could die at any time. Everyone knew but me. She wanted me to go to Colorado. I remember, while I was on the train, hearing the wheels of the train speeding very fast over the rails and thinking, "I should not be going. I should have stayed home."

When we arrived in Colorado, I was amazed at the huge, beautiful mountains. We all had to register. There was a long line of teens in a line. When I told them my name, the pastors all looked up and one of them took me aside. He told me that my mother had died. They flew me home.

My eldest sister Eleanor had an old friend who, out of the blue, called her one evening. She said she had not talked to her for a long time. My sister shared with her that I was looking for a job. She told my sister that I needed to meet Bud Dykstra. He was a Christian and vice president of the Union Realty Mortgage Company in Chicago. I had an interview with Mr. Dykstra but he said he was not hiring. He then said "I feel that the Lord wants me to hire you." After graduating from Fenger High School, I immediately began working for them, typing mortgage papers and letters. I also relieved the switchboard operator when she went on break. Mr. Dykstra would come over and lean on the switchboard and talk to me. One day he said, "I know the man you're going to marry." One Saturday, he actually called me at home and said "I want you to be in my church tomorrow night to meet Ron."

Eleanor and Ted drove me to his church in South Holland and I met Ron Hill. Sure enough, Mr. Dykstra was right. One year later Ron and I were married on October 7, 1961.

I have fond memories of The Cedar Lake Christian Conference Grounds, in Cedar Lake, Indiana. I remember the bell ringing when the services were about to begin. Then, after the evening services, we would often go to the Candy Cabin for the best ice cream cones you could ever eat.

Eleanor and her husband Ted had a cottage there on the grounds. Our family spent many happy days and nights there. My brother-in-law, John would fix breakfast for all of us and would prepare our eggs just the way we liked them.

I think I was about 14 years old when I wrote this poem about the "Twin Oaks," at Cedar Lake:

**Twin Oaks**

The summers we spent in old Twin Oaks
Are truly remembered by all the folks
Its big cozy porch and living room too
Will remain in our hearts
Throughout the years through.
It will always seem strange
When we visit the Lake
To no longer be privileged to enter the gate
Although other folks will be dwelling therein
Our hearts will go out never to end.

It is my desire for many people to come to the saving knowledge of the Lord Jesus Christ. All glory to God, for allowing me to put many of His teachings in poetical form. I pray that the poems and prayers featured in *Feeding in His Pasture* will be a blessing to many and a source for multitudes to grow and love our Savior, the Lord Jesus Christ.

In Christ,
*Audrey Hill*

# CHAPTER 1
# BLESSINGS

Composed November 8, 1999

## Ashamed

Lord, I am learning more each day,
As around me the world I see,
Needs of men are very real,
How thankful I should be.

When I awake with each new dawn,
I may have if I wish,
An egg and toast and cereal too,
While children hold an empty dish.

A Turkish cloth, warm water too,
A scented bar of soap,
So many live in filth and rags,
Without a ray of hope.

A change of clothes, a pair of shoes,
A hairbrush and a comb,
While millions live right on the street,
Without a place called home.

When my day is gone, I lie to rest,
My bed is soft and clean,
And often think of those far off,
In a dark and dismal scene.

They dread to face another day
With all its grief and pain.
I am so blessed, so rich, oh Lord
And ashamed that I complain.

*Romans 8:28 (KJV)*
*And we know that all things work together for good to them that love God,*
*to them who are the called according to His purpose.*

Composed May 3, 1998

# Grow Where You're Planted

I must grow where I am planted,
This the word that comes to me,
And I'll trust Him for the harvest
He will send for all to see.

I may wish I had been planted
In some richer soil somewhere,
But I look around and notice
He's now planting everywhere.

He will feed me on the manna
Sent fresh daily from above,
And the endless showers of blessing
Will remind me of His love.

I may then enrich the soil
And see others also blessed,
I'll continue to grow deeper
As I lean on Him for rest.

*Jeremiah 17:7 (NKJV)*
*Blessed is the man who trusts in the LORD,*
*and whose hope is the LORD.*

# Sweet Liberty

Free to worship,
Free to pray,
Free to raise
My hands today.

Free to love you,
Free to care,
No yoke of bondage
Will I bear,

The Holy Spirit
Residing in me
Reveals the Father
And Jesus to me,

Higher and higher
He keeps lifting me
Into new realms
Of intimacy,

Oh, glorious fulfillment,
Oh, great ecstasy,
Experiencing freedom
And sweet liberty.

*Galatians 5:1 (NKJV)*
*Stand fast therefore in the liberty by which Christ has made us free,*
*and do not be entangled again with a yoke of bondage.*

# Treasures

The things I find in pockets
Of my seven-year-old boy,
To him are loved and treasured
As his most expensive toy.

Old papers, plastic objects,
Rusty screws, they mean a lot;
But at times I must discard it,
Lest it pile up and rot.

Does my Heavenly Father shake His head,
Or maybe shed a tear,
When He sees His blood-bought children
Collecting junk down here?

He wants to shower His blessings,
In a most abundant way;
But our hands hold tight to "treasures,"
That will rust and then decay.

**Matthew 6:21 (NKJV)**
*For where your treasure is there will your heart be also.*

Composed October 17, 2015

## Five Minutes too Late

We do not know
What soon shall be,
Signs of the times
We clearly see.

Time as we know it
Will suddenly end,
God only knows
What lies 'round the bend.

Make sure you're ready,
Do not hesitate,
It's better to be early
Than five minutes too late.

*1 Thessalonians 5:7 (KJV)*
*For yourselves know perfectly*
*that the day of the Lord so cometh*
*as a thief in the night.*

Composed July 30, 2006

# Gather My Children

Let the bride come together
In spirit and truth,
This was His plan from the start.
He filled her again and again with His love,
Let her express her heart.

Let her sing, let her sing,
Let her sing His song,
His angels will one day appear,
With sickle in hand, they will go through the fields
And reap with a vengeance strong.

They have an assignment
That will be carried out;
Separate the wheat from the tares,
Burn the tares in the fire,
And carefully lift and
Gather My children, My Heirs.

*Matthew 24:31 (NKJV)*
*And He will send His angels with a great sound of a trumpet,*
*and they will gather together His elect from the four winds,*
*from one end of heaven to the other.*

Composed October 18, 1998

# Prepare

Reveal who You are Lord Jesus,
Reveal who You are.
Send Your light and strong conviction –
Pierce through every hardened scar.

Break through coldness and indifference,
Break through mediocrity,
Break down walls we all have mortared,
By our pride and piety.

Let our eyes see Jesus only,
Let our ears hear your small voice.
Let our hearts break deep within us,
Cause our spirits to rejoice.

Holy Spirit do whatever,
Burn away the chaff and dross,
Draw us back again to Calvary –
Keep us near the blood-stained cross.

Let the bells of freedom thunder,
Let us hear a clarion call,
Let us know Your "full salvation"
Available for one and all.

In Jesus' Name, oh let this happen,
Stop the mean and vicious lies,
Prepare oh the bride of Christ to meet Him –
We soon will see Him in the skies.

*1 John 3:2 (NKJV)*
*Beloved, now we are children of God;*
*and it has not yet been revealed what we shall be,*
*but we know that when He is revealed,*
*we shall be like Him, for we shall see Him as He is.*

Composed November 2010

# He Will Return

Angels announced to the shepherds,
Jesus' glorious birth,
Angels appeared to the disciples,
When Jesus ascended the earth.

This very same Jesus will descend with a shout
The archangel will be heard loud and clear,
The trumpet of God will sound from the sky;
His appearing is drawing near.

*1 Thessalonians 4:16 (NASB95)*
*For the Lord himself shall descend*
*from heaven with a shout,*
*with the voice of the archangel,*
*and with the trump of God:*
*and the dead in Christ will rise first.*

Composed November 5, 1997

# The Coming of the Lord

The leaves are falling, skies are growing dark,
The robins are on their way south,
Bitter, harsh winds begin to blow;
Winter's about to embark.

The days of grace are flying by fast,
Signs of the end are here.
What glorious and grand proclamation –
The coming of the Lord is near!

*Matthew 24:3 (NKJV)*
*Now as He sat on the Mount of Olives,*
*the disciples came to Him privately, saying,*
*"Tell us, when will these things be?*
*And what will be the sign of Your coming,*
*and of the end of the age?"*

Composed April 7, 1994

# Winds of Hell

The lamp in the temple has almost gone out,
The columns stand hollow and cold,
Many words echo forth without Spirit and power,
The sheep food is lifeless and old.

The winds of hell blow in through the walls,
There's no safety, the door has no lock;
False shepherds have come and led many astray,
They have scattered and wounded His flock.

He will come with a vengeance, the fire will fall,
It will be a most dreadful hour.
The day of the Lord is about to begin
And the true church will rise up in power.

The Ancient of Days has been refining gold
His work will soon be unveiled
Intercessory prayers of the faithful saints
Have been heard and they have prevailed.

*Ezekiel 34:2,3,5,6,12,13, 30,31 (NKJV)*

*Thus says the Lord God to the shepherds, "Woe to the shepherds of Israel... you do not feed the flock. They were scattered because there was no shepherd. My flock was scattered over the whole face of the Earth. As a shepherd seeks out his flock on the day he is among his scattered sheep, so will I seek out My sheep and deliver them. "And I will bring them out from the peoples and gather them from the countries, and will bring them to their own land; I will feed them. Thus they shall know that I, the LORD their God, am with them, and they, the house of Israel, are My people," says the Lord GOD. "You are My flock, the flock of My pasture; you are men, and I am your God," says the Lord GOD.*

# CHRISTIAN LIFE

Composed June 8, 1991

## Last Straw

May I not be the one
To add the last straw
To the load of my brother
And cause him to fall.

*Romans 14:13 (KJV)*
*Let us not therefore judge one another anymore: but judge this rather,*
*that no man put a stumbling or an occasion to fall in his brother's way.*

## My Desire

I want to trust Him here below,
I want to serve Him as I go,
I want to read His Word and grow,
I want for many more to know.

*Psalms 45:1 (KJV)*
*My heart is overflowing with a beautiful thought!*
*I will write a lovely poem to the King.*

Composed February 26, 1993

# New Wine

Walking on top of the water,
No drug can produce such a high.
Soaring into the heavenlies,
For one taste of this wine I would die.

The brand is called "Life in The Spirit,"
It is wild, very bubbly and pure.
The more that I drink, the more that I live,
Every problem I have this will cure.

I get drunk on the wine of the Spirit,
I am ruined for the things here and now;
As I look all around in the natural,
It is garbage just fit for a sow.

I am drawn back again to His winery,
The essence is so very fine;
I'll draw deep from the wells of salvation,
For another taste of new wine.

He has saved the best 'till now.

*Psalm 34:8 (KJV)*
*O taste and see that the Lord is good:*
*blessed is the man that trusteth in Him.*

Composed January 27. 1993

# One With Jesus

One with God the Father
Drawing closer every day
Becoming one with Jesus
As I let Him have His way.

*John 17:21-23 (KJV)*

*That they all may be one; as thou, Father, art in Me, and I in thee, that they also may be one in us: that the world may believe that thou has sent Me. And the glory which thou gavest Me I have given them; that they may be one, even as we are one: I in them, and thou in Me, that they may be made perfect in one; and that the world may know that thou hast sent Me, and hast loved them, as thou hast loved Me.*

# Satan

A wily ol' serpent,
The father of lies,
He subtlety comes
In a clever disguise.
He traps, then enjoys
The heart wrenching cries,
And laughs while his victim
Suffers and dies.

▶ Satan attacking his foes, Grace and Justice

*1 Peter 5:8 (NKJV)*
*Be sober, be vigilant;*
*because your adversary the devil walks about like a roaring lion,*
*seeking whom he may devour.*

Composed April 7, 2000

# Victory

When I decide to cross the "I"
And make the "I" a "T,"
I find complete fulfillment
And see the victory.

For every victory I see
I must decide to die,
As I humble myself
In the sight of the Lord,
He then comes, and lifts me high.

*Galatians 2:20 (KJV)*

*I am crucified with Christ nevertheless I live; yet not I but Christ liveth in me: and the
life which I now live by the flesh I live by the faith of the Son of God, who loved me,
and gave Himself for me.*

Joseph and Mary being told by the innkeeper that there is
no room except back in the barn with the animals

**CHAPTER 2**
# CHRISTMAS

## A Savior

They came at last to Bethlehem
Hungry, tired and worn,
Mary and Joseph had come so far,
Now Jesus would soon be born.

She needed care and attention,
Joseph could not find a place,
The inns were all filled,
He continued to knock
But every door was closed in his face.

"Wait – come back, there's a place out in back.
I'll bring you out some clean hay.
It's all that I have to offer,
It's where the animals stay."

Joseph and Mary walked to the back,
No other place could be found.
Amidst the filth and squalor
He helped her down to the ground.

In the still of the night a baby boy was born,
A beautiful, beautiful boy.
Mary looked long at her precious son;
He would bring unspeakable joy.

He came from glory and splendor,
God's Son, on a bed of hay,
For us He went to Calvary,
We have a Savior today.

*Luke 2:11 (NKJV)*
*"For there is born to you this day*
*in the city of David a Savior, who is Christ the Lord.*

# Bethlehem

"Oh little town of Bethlehem"
So small, so insignificant,
But, God ordained that His Son
Be born in you.

"Yet in your dark streets shineth,
The everlasting light,"
Yes! Hallelujah! Glory to God!
You have been born in me.

You have brought great light
Into the deep, dark crevices of my heart,
Great joy, indescribable peace and
Divine satisfaction has followed.

"The hopes and fears of all the years
Are met in thee tonight."
For unto me has been born a Savior,
Jesus Christ The Lord.

I am "Bethlehem"

*Micah 5:2 (NKJV)*
*But you, Bethlehem Ephrathah,*
*though you are little among the thousands of Judah,*
*Yet out of you shall come forth to Me the One to be Ruler in Israel,*
*Whose goings forth are from of old, from everlasting.*

# Emmanuel

Emmanuel, Emmanuel,
His name is called Emmanuel,
God with us, revealed in us,
His name is called Emmanuel.

*Matthew 1:23 (KJV)*
*Behold, a virgin shall be with child, and shall bring forth a son, and they shall call his*
*name Emmanuel, which being interpreted is, God with us.*

# God's Gift of the Ages

What were the thoughts of the Father
As He watched His son being born;
When He laid His Son in the arms of the world
That very first Christmas morn?

What were the thoughts of the Father
When we plunged the spear in His side;
When we nailed His hands and feet to the cross
And Jesus yielded His Spirit and died?

Turn off the Christmas tree, lay the wrappings aside,
Stop for a moment, we must take a ride,
We won't go first class and we won't need much fuel,
We'll be riding today on the back of a mule.

Enter into the stable, look down where He lay,
This is God's Son in this manger of hay,
Now approaching Mt. Calvary, stand here and gaze,
With tears falling fast, we fall to our knees.

At the 'Place of a Skull,' Christ died on a tree,
The scenes that we saw were not pretty to see,
But we must travel back; we must turn back the pages,
And reflect once again on God's gift of the ages.

*II Corinthians 9:15 (NIV)*
*Thanks be to God*
*for his indescribable gift.*

Composed December 18, 1994

## God's Precious Gift

From the manger's
Gentle bed of straw
To Calvary's hill
Of bitter gall,
So great
A sacrifice was made
So great a love,
My ransom paid.

*Matthew 20:28 (NASB95)*
*Just as the Son of Man did not come to be served,*
*but to serve, and to give His life a ransom for many.*

## It Isn't

It isn't the gifts, it isn't the snow,
It isn't the lovely candles that glow,
It isn't the food, it isn't the lights,
It isn't the breathtaking spectacular sights,
We needed a Savior, He came from above,
Christmas truly is a story of love.

*Luke 2:11 (NASB95)*
*...for today in the city of David*
*there has been born for you a Savior,*
*who is Christ the Lord.*

# His Gift

There is a gift sent from above,
It's tagged, "From God to You, With love."
A gift for me? A twinkling star?
Oh no, oh no, much more by far.

His precious gift lies on the straw
In Bethlehem, in yonder stall.
His blood will flow for all to see,
On down the road at Calvary.

Amazing gift how can this be,
That God would give Himself for me?
What kind of gift do I return?
What must I pay? How can I earn?

"Eternal Life" through Christ the Lord
You cannot pay, nor can afford.
This gift for you on a bed of straw,
Demands your heart, your life, your all.

*Romans 6:23 (KJV)*
*For the wages of sin is death,*
*but the gift of God is eternal life*
*through Jesus Christ our Lord.*

Christmas '85

Composed December 2011

## Jesus is the Light of the World

On that night long ago,
One bright star guided the wise men
To the manger.

In this present darkness
There is only one bright star
We can follow. He is
"The Bright and Morning Star."

Follow Jesus,
Find Love, Joy and Peace.

*John 8:12 (KJV)*
*I am the light of the world;*
*He that followeth me shall not walk in darkness,*
*but shall have the light of life.*

## No Room Today

If Jesus were here in person today,
The same One who way down in Bethlehem lay;
Would be welcomed and wanted by all,
Or again be pushed back in some animal stall?

Quickly, we answer, oh no, no indeed!
We'd make sure to provide for His every need;
We would stop all our work and give ear to His voice,
For the King would be here, we would greatly rejoice.

But I wonder today, as I look all around,
Almost nowhere this Christmas can Jesus be found.
How sad, sad indeed, on His own very day,
He is nearly forgotten and pushed out of the way.

But then in the distance, a carol I hear,
The strain is so lovely, the words are so dear;
I'm again filled with wonder, amazement and joy,
That man could meet God in a sweet baby boy.

*Luke 1:35 (NASB95)*
*The angel answered and said to her, "The Holy Spirit will come upon you,*
*and the power of the Most High will overshadow you;*
*and for that reason the holy Child shall be called the Son of God.*

## Thank You God

He would,
He would
Give you a gift
To show His love
To bring you joy,

He did,
He gave
His very best,
This one,
This only
Precious boy.

*Romans 6:23 (KJV)*
*For the wages of sin is death;*
*but the gift of God is eternal life through Jesus Christ our Lord.*

## The First Christmas

The sky was a mass of diamonds,
It was a beautiful quiet night,
The shepherds kept watch in the fields
Drenched in the pale moonlight.

Suddenly the silence was broken,
A bright light shone all around;
An angel had an announcement
For the shepherds on the ground.

"Jesus is born in Bethlehem"
An angelic choir sang;
"Glory to God in the highest,
Peace on earth," the chorus rang.

A great star shone over the stable,
They found Him there in the hay,
So filled with joy and amazement,
This was the first Christmas day.

*Luke 2:13, 14 (KJV)*

*And suddenly there was with the angel a multitude of the heavenly host praising God and saying: "Glory to God in the highest, and on earth peace, goodwill toward men!"*

# The Forgotten Tree

As Christmas time approaches
There is much activity
Among the things that we must do
We must find that perfect tree.

We bring it home and set it up
In a place for all to see,
Bright lights, expensive ornaments
Create a Christmas tree.

This tree, so very beautiful
But before my very eyes
I see needles start to fall
It soon dries up and dies.

To many lovely Christmas trees
We see all through the season
And hear that old familiar phrase that
"Jesus is the reason."

There is an old forgotten tree
Not lovely to behold
It reveals the ugliness of sin
Jesus bore the awful load.

This rugged, old forgotten tree
Held the Light of all the world
Lifted up for us to see
A display of love unfurled.

This is, this is the most beautiful tree
A most glorious message relayed
"This is the reason I have come,
"Believe, your redemption is paid."

*Galatians 3:13 (KJV)*

*Christ redeemed us from the curse of the Law, having become a curse for us—for it is written, "CURSED IS EVERYONE WHO HANGS ON A TREE."*

## The Message

Snowflakes softly falling,
Blanketing.
Christmas carols fill the air,
How beautiful they sound.
Listen closely to their message –
The words are so profound,
God's son was born in Bethlehem,
In a manger He was found.

*Luke 2:7 (NKJV)*
*And she brought forth her firstborn Son, and wrapped Him in swaddling cloths and*
*laid Him in a manger, because there was no room for them in the inn.*

# The Price That Was Paid

How traditional and lovely
To gather 'round the hearth
And read the Christmas story
How Jesus left heaven for earth.

Maybe it's just a story to you
About a sweet little babe in a stable,
Or maybe it's just time to enjoy
And feast from a bountiful table.

We stop and celebrate Christmas
But it is more, it is more, so much more,
Consider the gift that was given
As you hang the wreath on your door.

Have you walked the long road to Calvary
To see the price that was paid?
Your eternal destiny was at stake;
No lesser payment He made.

If you walk away, cold and indifferent
If this does not change you within,
To whom will you go for salvation?
There is no atonement for sin.

Do you know Him as personal Savior?
Have you accepted Him into your heart?
Or will He say, as He looks into your eyes –
"I never knew you, depart!"

You may gain the whole world and lose your soul;
What profit, what profit is there?
Do not neglect the gift of salvation,
Take time, take time to prepare.

A new year will soon be upon us,
Time is fleeting away,
The signs Jesus spoke of are all present –
This could be the last Christmas day.

## The Star of Bethlehem

"Do you hear what I hear?"
The star, the star and all of its glory,
The manger, wisemen and shepherds
Have been replaced with a different story.

It's all about Santa, reindeer and a sleigh,
Much shopping and parties a must,
While The Book that tells the true story
Lies forgotten and buried in dust.

But this very same Jesus
Will break through the blue,
We do not know the hour when,
The true star of Christmas
Will appear in the clouds –
Jesus is coming again!

Composed December 2004

# What is Beautiful is a Joy for All Seasons

Enter into the joy
Of this beautiful season,
God came to earth
And we were the reason.

Jesus our Savior was born Christmas day,
There is joy for all seasons,
There is hope come what may.

*Luke 2:8-9 (NASB95)*
*In the same region there were some shepherds staying*
*out in the fields and keeping watch over their flock by night.*
*And an angel of the Lord suddenly stood before them,*
*and the glory of the Lord shone around them;*
*and they were terribly frightened.*

Composed July 8, 1998

# What Wondrous Love is This

The greatest event of all time and space,
Was when God came and died for the human race.

The Love of God we would never know
If God had not come to earth below.

An act of love the greatest display,
God in flesh on a bed of hay.

He left through gates of splendor,
To earth as an infant, so tender,
He became our glorious Savior.

*John 6:38 (NASB95)*
*For I came down from heaven,*
*not to do my own will,*
*but the will of him that sent me.*

# Where Else?

Born among cattle,
Filth and flies,
A perfect and spotless
Little lamb lies.

The angels announced
His miraculous birth,
Singing, proclaiming –
"Peace and joy to the earth!"

The shepherds and wise men
Came from afar,
To come and adore the lamb
Led by a star.

The lamb was God's Son,
The Lord Jesus Christ,
Given for us,
God's supreme sacrifice.

Why in a stable,
Not a palace
On that first Christmas morn?
Think again, just where else
Would a lamb be born?

*Luke 2:14 (KJV)*
*"Glory to God in the highest,
and on earth peace among men
with whom He is pleased."*

# Why?

God has no depth, no width, no height,
Was found in a manger one starry night.
God is bigger than the universe,
Was nailed to a cross becoming a curse.

Look in the manger, gaze at the cross,
Silently ask yourself, "Why?"
He is asking those who casually gaze,
"Is it nothing to you who pass by?"

**Colossians 1:16 (NASB95)**

*For by Him all things were created, both in the heavens and on earth, visible and invisible, whether thrones or dominions or rulers or authorities—all things have been created through Him and for Him.*

# CHAPTER 3
# COMFORT

## He Knew My Name

I know just what you're going through,
Sincere folks sometimes say,
But they can only sympathize,
We all come a different way.

Your path may be more winding,
While mine is rough and steep,
Still others live on mountain tops,
Or in valleys dark and deep.

No two people are the same,
We're all different as can be,
And only Jesus knows my path,
He knows the real me.

He only knows about the tears
I shed when no one sees,
He knows my heart, my joy, my needs,
He cares and intercedes

Oh, what a comfort to my heart
To know He knows my frame,
Before He made the world with words,
Praise God, He knew my name.

*Psalm 103:14 (KJV)*
*For He knoweth our frame; He remembereth that we are dust.*

Composed March 15, 1993

# Know the Lord

I know who You are Lord,
I know who You are;
In my spirit I know You
Oh bright morning star.

Earth trembles and shakes
At the sound of Your voice,
But knowing You Jesus
Makes my spirit rejoice.

I do not fear evil,
No, not even death,
For You are so near Lord,
As near as my breath.

*1 John 4:18 (KJV)*
*There is no fear in love;*
*but perfect love casteth out fear:*
*because fear has torment.*
*He that feareth is not made perfect in love.*

Composed April 12, 1991

# Clouds

"When I am hurting deep within,
And I do not feel You near,
Where do I turn, where do I run
When my mind is filled with fear?"

"I lay here captive in my bed,
What would You have me to do?
My Creator, Lord and Savior,
I would be true to you."

"Relinquish all to Me my child,
Draw closer to My side,
Cry out to Me in all your pain –
It is for this I died."

"Today you do not understand
This pain and suffering,
But lift it, lift it up to Me,
My love and peace I'll bring."

"I am the Master Potter,
You are "My" piece of clay,
I am molding out a masterpiece;
This is the only way."

"You will come forth as gold refined,
A treasure to behold,
Only trust Me in the furnace,
Do not resist the mold."

"Do not let clouds get in the way
In the quiet, calm and still,
As you draw closer, to Me,
You will know my perfect will."

*2 Corinthians 1:5 (NIV)*
*For just as we share abundantly in the sufferings of Christ, so also our comfort*
*abounds through Christ.*

November 11, 1989

# He Meets Me There

No one knows when I am hurting,
Crying out with upraised hands,
He swiftly comes and re-assures me –
He completely understands.

No one knows how much I love Him,
No one knows how much I care;
No one knows how sweet our meeting,
Our quiet place, He meets me there.

He truly is The Great "I AM" to me.

My Deliverer, my Fortress, my Helper
My Defense, my Strength, my Rock,
My Comforter, my...
Hallelujah! I praise Him.

*2 Corinthians 1:3 (NKJV)*
*Blessed be the God and Father of our Lord Jesus Christ,*
*the Father of mercies and God of all comfort.*

# Higher Still

High, so very high in God,
Delighting in His will,
Believing I have reached the peak,
He lifts me higher still.

*Psalm 61:1-2 (KJV)*
*Hear my cry, O God; attend unto my prayer.*
*From the end of the earth will I cry unto thee,*
*when my heart is overwhelmed:*
*lead me to the rock that is higher than I.*

Composed June 16, 1998

# Jesus Wasn't too Busy

Jesus wasn't too busy to heal the sick,
He made the lame to walk,
He cleansed the leper's putrid sores,
Helped those who couldn't talk.

Jesus wasn't too busy to stop for a man
Who was hated and dreaded by all;
Zacchaeus his name, was noticed by Him,
Even though his stature was small.

Jesus wasn't too busy to pour out His life;
He left his Father on high,
He knew the value and worth of one soul,
And He asks me the question – do I?

Jesus wasn't too busy and He hasn't changed;
He's the same as He was long ago,
We can go to Him now with burdens we bear,
He still loves and will mercy bestow.

*Matthew 11:28 (NASB95)*
*"Come to Me, all who are weary and heavy-laden,*
*and I will give you rest.*

Composed December 26, 2002

# Midst of Me

God is in the midst of me,
I'm overflowing and filled to the brim.
His love is the joy and strength of my life,
Each day I learn more of Him.

God is in the midst of me,
In the center, in the core of my being.
A vessel, His temple, filled with His love,
May I never prevent others from seeing.

May my spirit like a candle,
Have a beautiful glow,
Drawing people to Jesus,
So they too will know.

*Ephesians 5:18 (KJV)*
*And be not drunk with wine, wherein is excess; but be filled with the Spirit.*

Composed March 12, 2005

# Sleep

My sleep is so sweet
With You ever near,
I'm free from all anxiousness,
Worry and fear.
Your presence is with me
Throughout the still night,
Oh God, I am never
Out of Your sight.

*Jeremiah 31:25,26 (NKJV)*
*"For I have satiated the weary soul, and I have replenished every sorrowful soul."*
*After this I awoke and looked around, and my sleep was sweet to me.*

Composed April 9, 2001

# Never Forsaken

"I will never leave you nor forsake you."
But how close are you, my Lord?
"How close is the fragrance to the rose?"
I would think,
That it is in the very core of the rose,
"So it is with you and Me."

# When You Fall in Love

When you fall in love with Jesus,
It's so easy to obey;
It becomes a joy to witness
And to read His Word and pray.

When He fills you with His Spirit
And you feel His presence near,
It's mountaintop experience,
Just a taste of heaven here.

Jesus is the joy of living,
When He lives within your heart;
You will sense a river flowing
And Jesus never will depart.

For the more you get to know Him,
More like Him you'll want to be,
And the best is yet before us,
When His lovely face we see.

*2 Corinthians 1:3 (NKJV)*
*Blessed be the God and Father of our Lord Jesus Christ,*
*the Father of mercies and God of all comfort.*

# COMPASSION

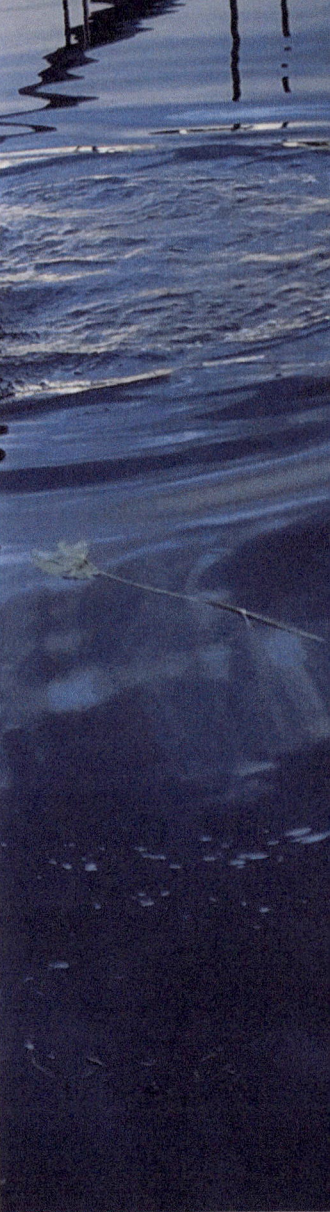

## Broken Heart

Has your heart been truly broken
By His love and tender care?
Do you ever cry for others
That are hurting everywhere?

A broken heart will never hold
Unforgiveness or a grudge;
You'll be moved with deep compassion
By the Spirit's gentle nudge.

We hear and read so much of love,
Still many of us lack;
Instead of lifting burdens,
We add more sorrow to their back.

It's when your load's been lifted,
When you yourself are free;
That's when His love will overflow
In glorious victory.

He needs more broken hearts today,
Flowing free with love and grace.
Reaching out to all who suffer,
Healing wounds to every place.

*Psalm 51:17 (KJV)*
*The sacrifices of God are a broken spirit:*
*a broken and contrite heart, O God, thou will not despise .*

Composed January 12, 2004

## Greatest Need

What was your greatest need today?
Jesus Christ is greater,
He would draw you to Himself today,
Jesus Christ is greater.

He will meet your very deepest need,
Place your feet on solid rock.
He is standing at your heart's door,
Be still and hear Him knock.

In faith believe and trust His Word,
You need not wait 'til later,
He'll meet you where you are right now,
Jesus Christ is greater.

**Proverbs 3:5 (KJV)**
*Trust in the Lord with all thine heart:*
*and lean not unto thine own understanding.*

# CHAPTER 4
# CREATION

Composed April 9, 2005

## Above All

How can I possibly know God,
How do I approach His throne?
He is bigger than the universe;
He is God and God alone.

I can hear His love in the morning
In the gentle coo of a dove,
And I see His power in creation
As I gaze at the heavens above.

But to really know God as my Creator,
To know what lies deep in His heart,
I must go to the pages of scripture,
This is the place I must start.

His love is unraveled in scripture,
I see Jesus, a servant of all,
God in flesh walking among us,
I see Love, I see Love above all.

*Colossians 1:17 (KJV)*
*And he is before all things, and by him all things consist.*

Composed June 28, 2001

# A Feather

A fragile feather
Fell off a little bird,
It laid for several hours
But no one saw or heard.

One day a man came walking
Along the dusty path.
He notices the lovely feather
And wondered as in the past.

"Why do I pick up feathers"
While most would just discard,
This fragile, gentle beauty
Of the feather and this man,
Are seldom ever noticed
As fine, soft drifting sand.

*Psalm 91:4 (NKJV)*
*He shall cover you with His feathers,*
*And under His wings you shall take refuge;*
*His truth shall be your shield and buckler.*

Composed October 12, 1999

# If Ever I would Leave You

If ever I would leave you, it wouldn't be in summer.
Seeing you in summer, I never would go,
Your hair streaked with sunlight, your lips red as flame,
Your face with a luster that puts gold to shame.

But if I'd ever leave you, it couldn't be in autumn.
How I'd leave in autumn, I will never know,
I've seen how you sparkle when fall nips the air,
I know you in autumn and I must be there.

And could I leave you running merrily through the snow?
Or on a wintry evening when you catch the fire's glow?

If ever I would leave you, how could it be in springtime?
Knowing how spring I'm in awe of you so.
Oh, no, not in springtime, summer, winter or fall,
No never could I leave you at all.

*2 Timothy 4:7 (NIV)*
*I have fought the good fight,*
*I have finished the race,*
*I have kept the faith.*

# SEASONS – SPRING

## First Breath of Spring

We're all so thankful this year for spring;
The return of the birds and the song that they sing,
After winters' harsh winds and those long, cold, dark days,
With great joy we welcome the sun's wonderful rays.

We're so glad that the winter is now in the past
And we hope we have felt the last arctic blast;
But ol' man winter just hates to give up,
Until every drop is drained from his cup.

But we've hung in this far and it's great just to know
We've got summer ahead with no ice, sleet or snow;
With the first breath of spring, we're already revived,
Spring re-affirms God is truly alive.

*Isaiah 61:11 (KJV)*
*For as the earth bringeth forth her bud, and as the garden causeth the things that*
*are sown in it to spring forth; so the Lord GOD will cause righteousness*
*and praise to spring forth before all the nations.*

## August

Hot and humid days of August,
Nights are balmy, warm and fair.
Butterflies fly in the sunshine,
Sounds of insects fill the air.

A somber, melancholy feeling
Always comes this time of year.
When I see the days get shorter;
I know that fall is drawing near.

Canning season's almost over,
Enough for us and some to spare.
School supplies must soon be purchased;
A sad excitement fills the air.

Robins too, begin to gather,
How we'll miss their lifting song.
All too soon the leaves turn crimson,
All too soon sweet summers gone.

*Philippians 4:19 (KJV)*
*But my God shall supply all your need*
*according to his riches in glory by Christ Jesus.*

Composed May 7, 1998

# Beyond the Night Sky

One night when I was just a child
My daddy said to me,
"Come and let's go out of doors,
There's something you must see."

Together we stood there in the yard
And he said, "Look and see the heavens,"
I said, "Okay but why?"

"God made all those twinkling stars,
There are many you can't see,
He's the God of all creation,
And He made both you and me."

There was something that swept over me,
A sweetness filled the air,
I sensed the awesomeness of God
As we stood together there.

*Genesis 1:16 (KJV)*
*And God made two great lights; the greater light to rule the day,*
*and the lesser light to rule the night: He made the stars also.*

Seasons

Composed September 1, 1996

# God Is Love

One morning while out picking berries,
I stopped to examine a flower,
I examined every detail
And reflected again on God's power.

I continued on picking berries
Enjoying the fresh summer air,
I sensed an awareness of Jesus
There in the garden so fair.

There aren't any words in our language
To describe all His gifts from above,
But even in one little flower
We can see God is good, God is love.

*James 1:17 (NKJV)*

*Every good gift and every perfect gift is from above, and comes down from the*
*Father of lights, with whom there is no variation or shadow of turning.*

# What Value

You built lofty places in the heavens;
You set forth the foundations of earth.
You called the oceans and seas to come forth,
And You stooped to so lowly a birth?
I am only a speck of dust,
What value, what is it You see?
"You are made in the image of Me."

*Genesis 1:27 (NKJV)*

*God created man in His own image, in the image of God He created him;*
*male and female He created them.*

# Leaving the Nest

Have you ever watched a mother bird
Push her offspring from the nest?
While most of her young were eager to fly,
One was shyer than the rest.

You could feel the fear that the young bird felt
As you watched this tenseful scene
He had been so secure, but now he thought
"Why is Mama being so mean?"

He began to fall but quickly spread
His tiny wings to fly.
Afraid at first and yes, he thought
That he would surely die.

But suddenly he felt his wings
Lift him high into the sky;
He was learning how to fly at last.
And Mama breathed a sigh.

*Job 39:26 (NKJV)*
*Does the hawk fly by your wisdom,*
*And spread its wings toward the south?*

Composed July 8, 1991

# Little Bird

He sent a little bird
To sing his song for me,
It opened wide the floodgates
And set my spirit free.

*Job 35:10 (KJV)*
*But none saith, where is God my maker, who giveth songs in the night.*

Composed March 20, 1995

# My God

My God is so holy, so mighty, so strong –
Can give to a robin a sweet lifting song;
He causes the earth to tremble and shake,
And yet a small playful kitten can make.

He knows the number of hairs on my head,
And daily sees that the birds are all fed;
He creates and sustains and makes everything grow,
And causes the winds to howl and blow.

To stand before Him, I would tremble and fear,
But I know that Jesus will stand very near;
He's my Savior and friend and He died in my place,
I already know that He's won my case.

*Matthew 10:30 (KJV)*
*But the very hairs of your head are all numbered.*

## Last Days

The last days of summer are suddenly here,
And autumn with harvest draws somberly near;
The swimming and picnics, the great summer fun,
Is just about over when summer is done.

The long sunny days and the warm balmy nights;
The crickets and lightning bugs with bright blinking lights,
Will soon all be gone, once again in the past;
Like a beautiful sunset, how I wish it would last.

The garden-fresh vegetables, the tomatoes so red,
Must be gathered in quickly, soon the vines will be dead.
The windows and doors, we'll again have to close,
All too soon, Mr. Frost will be nipping on our nose.

Soon "time" as we know it will also be past,
And only what's done then for Jesus will last;
He's the Lord of the harvest and will judge us someday;
Will my works stand the test, or like chaff blow away?

*Matthew 9:38 (NASB95)*
*"Therefore beseech the Lord of the harvest*
*to send out workers into His harvest."*

## Winter

Crystal clear, long quiet nights,
Bitter winds that sting and bite;
Snow and ice chunk under foot,
Rug gets soiled from chimney soot.

Red birds in the evergreens,
One of winter's lovely scenes;
Sun is sinking, big and red,
Landscape barren, grey and dead.

Inside, it is safe and warm,
Bar the door from winters' storm;
Food on the shelves that can't be beat,
Gathered in the summers' heat.

Blankets piled high upon the beds,
Mittens, scarves and bright red sleds;
Stiff and sore cold hands and feet
From the bitter wind and sleet.

Snow piled high outside of the door,
Someone says, "We'll soon have more."
Bleak and lonely time of year,
I'm glad that spring is drawing near.

*Psalm 148:8 (NASB95)*
*Fire and hail, snow and clouds; Stormy wind, fulfilling His Word.*

Composed January 16, 1986

## Snow

How beautiful new fallen snow,
So soft, so fresh and clean.
How magnificent You are oh Lord,
To create this lovely scene,

How beautiful we are to You,
We're whiter than the snow,
A glorious church; all sin is gone,
Washed in the crimson flow.

*Psalm 51:7 (NKJV)*
*Purge me with hyssop, and I shall be clean;*
*Wash me, and I shall be whiter than snow.*

# CROSS

## Crucifixion

Could you stand it if they spit on you,
If they angrily pulled out your hair,
Could you stand the nails in your hands and your feet;
Would you love them enough to hang there?

When you listen to false accusations,
Do you quietly let the tears flow,
Or in anger, lash out unlike Jesus,
Who chose to go down very low.

"They do not know what they're doing," He said,
They are blind and vainly deceived.
But do you love them enough to give up your life
So that others might see and believe?

He's creating a beautiful jewel in you,
And until all the chaff and the dross
Has been burned up with Holy Ghost fire,
Choose life, and remain on the cross.

*Luke 23:34 (KJV)*
*Then said Jesus, Father, forgive them;*
*for they know not what they do.*

# Dust

God, Creator of all,
Formed man out of the dust of the ground.
Man sinned.
"Without the shedding of blood,
There is no remission of sin."
God came down and became flesh.
Man hated Him without cause.
They beat His back with 39 stripes,
Placed a crown of thorns on His head,
Mocked Him, spit on Him and
Made Him carry His cross up Calvary's hill.
They nailed His hands and feet to a Roman cross.
They pierced His side with a sword.
After they vented their hatred and had done their worst,
"They sat down and watched Him there."
His blood flowing down the cross,
Streaming unto the dust of the earth.

*Genesis 2:7 (KJV)*
*And the LORD God formed man of the dust of the ground,*
*and breathed into his nostrils the breath of life; and man became a living soul*

Composed December 2006

# Experience the Wonder

Why did He come?
He was God,
He had no need,
But there was a tree in His future,
Because Love must be revealed.

After men had done their worst
And sealed Him in a grave,
He arose!
Because Love is victorious.

He's coming again!
For those He's redeemed,
He'll break through the blue
Because Love is glorious.

There are many crowns in His future
For the Lord Jesus Christ,
The King of Kings,
The Lord of Lords,
Because Love never fails.

*Revelation 14:14 (NKJV)*
*Then I looked, and behold, a white cloud, and on the cloud sat One like the Son of Man, having on His head a golden crown, and in His hand a sharp sickle.*

Composed January 25, 2000

# History's Saddest Hour

Long ago in eternity past
God had an idea when He created you,
Whether your eyes are chocolate brown,
Or beautiful indigo blue.

He carefully knit you together,
Every muscle, tissue and gland,
Like a potter who works with a piece of clay,
He fashions you with His hand.

You are one of a kind, you are very unique,
Your temperament, talent and style,
He is so very pleased with how He made you,
Down to your winning smile.

Like a lamb, how you needed a shepherd,
We are all so very prone,
To wander off into fields of sin,
All having a will of our own.

He came and He walked among us,
Healing and raising the dead,
God in the flesh, we despised Him,
Believing a lie instead.

At last we nailed Him to a Roman cross,
The hands that made our hands,
Then we lifted Him up for all to see,
His blood flowing out of the sands.

Savior, Redeemer, Creator of all,
He made every bird, tree and flower,
We rejected and killed the Author of Life –
This was history's saddest hour.

Forgive them, Father, forgive them,
He overcame evil with good,
We will never conceive the love of God,
It has never been understood.

*Acts 3:15 (NIV)*
*You killed the author of life.*

Composed March 11, 1999

# It is Finished

Nailed to a cross
My Redeemer died,
My salvation complete,
"It is finished," He cried.

"Redeemer, Redeemer,
How can it be?
Look again silly Christian,
He hangs dead on a tree."

"Wait Satan, wait,
As you laugh me to scorn,
Go to the garden scene
Next Sunday morn.

Look inside, look again,
See the place where He laid
He is gone, He is gone,
"My redemption is paid."

"I am doomed, I am doomed,
To my place I must go,
But I'm taking millions
To the portals below."

"I'll not go, I'll not go,
I'll not go with you,
I'm goin' up Satan,
Goin' up through the blue.

I will see, I will see,
I will soon see His face,
My Redeemer, my Savior,
Is preparin' a place.

*John 19:30 (KJV)*

*When Jesus therefore had received the vinegar, he said,*
*It is finished: and he bowed his head, and gave up the ghost.*

Composed April 23, 1993

# On the Tree

How much pride did Jesus have,
Hanging naked on the tree?
Oh Father God, there was no pride,
He was thinking then of me.

You placed my sin upon Him,
He shed His precious blood,
"Oh child stay here until the stream
Becomes the healing flood."

This flood of love and mercy,
Praise God, it covers me.
With Him I'm resurrected,
Forgiven, cleansed and free.

**1 Peter 2:24 (KJV)**
*Who his own self bare our sins in his own body on the tree, that we, being dead to sins, should live unto righteousness: by whose stripes ye were healed.*

# Pilate

Willing to content the crowd,
He let Barabbas go,
Then Jesus was delivered up
And the winds of Hell did blow.

They clothed Him in a purple robe,
Pressed thorns into His head,
Then mockingly they bowed their knees,
"King of the Jews!" they said.

How very sad to read these words,
They hurt and grieve our hearts,
To see how wicked man can be,
But did I play a part?

By simply keeping quiet,
I may too content the crowd,
Or by some sinful attitude,
My actions speak so loud.

So full of sin and selfishness,
We always want our way,
How we need the Holy Spirit
To live in power today.

*John 19:19 (KJV)*
*Pilate also wrote an inscription and put it on the cross. It was written,*
*"JESUS THE NAZARENE, THE KING OF THE JEWS."*

Composed September 12, 2002

## Scarred

They bound the hands of God with a chord,
Not knowing, not knowing that
He was the Lord,
Then they nailed His hands to a tree,
These wicked men
Were like you and me.

Our hearts are so wicked,
Our hearts are so hard,
His hands bear the nail prints
And will forever be scarred.

*John 20:25 (KJV)*

*The other disciples therefore said unto him, We have seen the Lord. But he said unto them, Except I shall see in his hands the print of the nails, and put my finger into the print of the nails, and thrust my hand into his side, I will not believe.*

# The Parting

I felt the Father's heart today
As I sat and read His Word,
It gripped my heart in such a way
As I had never heard.

I felt His love in just a measure
On that day they had to part,
When Jesus had to leave His Father,
How it tore and broke His heart.

Oh the pain of separation,
His loneliness was never eased,
"This is my Beloved Son,
In whom I am well pleased."

He let us kill and crucify Him,
He did not let His son go free,
Oh hear the dying cry of Jesus,
"Why have You forsaken Me?"

He turned His back on His Beloved,
He made a way for you and me,
Now Jesus pleads, with arms wide open,
"Come weary one, come unto me."

*Matthew 11:28 (NASB95)*
*"Come to Me, all who are weary and heavy-laden, and I will give you rest.*

# CHAPTER 5
# ETERNITY

Composed October 29, 1997

## Cries

A cry from the deep is building,
Intercession has been made through the years;
A cry, as it were, from a mother,
For her children, she sheds many tears.

A cry, a wail of anguish,
A cry from God's broken heart;
This cry is for mankind to know Him
Before He must say "Depart."

Today, His arms are wide open,
He yearns to give them His rest,
He desires to greatly fulfill them,
Holding them close to His breast.

Rejection, rejection, they still turn away,
Laughing, down the broad road,
Rejecting the One who would save them from hell,
Oblivious to their eternal abode.

In the ages to come, cries will be heard,
They'll experience all that they fear,
Too late, too late, their cries are too late!
In that day, He will turn a deaf ear.

*Revelation 20:15 (NIV)*
*Anyone whose name was not found written in the book of life*
*was thrown into the lake of fire.*

Composed July 14, 1996

# Dry Your Tears

It is always a shock
When a dear loved one dies,
We've often not said
Our final goodbyes.

When they're gone, it's too late
No more can we share,
When our loved one has breathed
Their last bit of air.

Death comes to all
But so hard to accept,
Jesus knew of our pain
For He also wept.

But it is not the end
If you've been reborn,
There's a reunion coming
One beautiful morn.

There will be no more parting
No more sadness or fears,
Heaven is waiting,
Dry, dry your tears.

**1 Corinthians 15:56 (KJV)**
*The sting of death is sin; and the strength of sin is the law.*

Composed May 16, 1986

## Final Rest

Farewell, sweet one, go take your flight,
To be received beyond this night.

You're gone from us, we miss you so,
You filled your place then had to go.

To be with Him who understood,
That you had done the best you could.

In heaven now you're with the Lord,
You see His face, this is your reward.

Lean precious lamb upon His breast,
He's called you to your final rest.

*1 Corinthians 15:56, 57 (KJV)*
*The sting of death is sin; and the strength of sin is the law.*
*But thanks be to God, which giveth us the victory through our Lord Jesus Christ.*

# Gettin' Ready

They're gettin' ready for battle,
They're gettin' ready for war.
The thing they fear will come upon them,
Then death and hell forevermore.

We're gettin' ready for glory;
Sometimes it's really hard to wait.
We'll be seein' all our loved ones,
They're prob'bly waitin' at the gate.

It won't be long now, just keep listenin'
For the trump of God to sound.
We'll be gone and they'll be sayin,'
"No trace of them can ere be found."

Don't look around here – look for Jesus!
He'll be breakin' through the blue;
Your reward is comin' shortly,
He's comin' back for me and you!

*1 Thessalonians 4:17 (KJV)*
*... and so shall we ever be with the Lord.*

# Heaven

Your eyes close in death and you're being lifted,
By a beautiful angel so big and so fair;
Inexpressible beauty you've never imagined,
Soft beautiful music is filling the air.

Into new realms lifted higher and higher;
All of life's cares are left far behind,
Eternal happiness, glory and splendor;
Fullness of joy and peace here you find.

You're now ushered into the presence of Jesus,
Loved ones and angels are all standing near;
"Welcome home, my dear child," He lovingly whispers,
And tenderly wipes away every tear.

**John 14:2 (KJV)**
*In my Father's house are many mansions:*
*if it were not so, I would have told you.*
*I go to prepare a place for you.*

# Hell

Your eyes close in death and you're plunging so swiftly;
A horrible feeling, that no words can tell.
Loud, torturous screams, in the inky thick blackness;
The demons await your arrival in hell.

You have perished forever, where Satan is captain;
No water is found and your tongue is so dry,
And then you begin to fall even further,
Down into the depths, "Oh help me!" you cry.

But God is not here, He won't even hear you;
The demons are mocking, instilling more fear.
The gnashing of teeth, in eternal darkness,
Forever forsaken from all that is dear.

**John 3:16 (KJV)**
*For God so loved the world, that He gave His only begotten son,*
*that whosoever believeth in Him should never perish,*
*but have everlasting life.*

Composed April 3, 2020

# Home at Last

We are standing,
We are shining,
We are all wearing white,
The darkness is gone –
We're in glorious light.

Heartache, separation,
Is all in the past,
We're singing, we're laughing –
We're together at last.

We're singing a new song
With no worry or fear,
We're rejoicing together –
He wiped away every tear.

Jesus came, Jesus bought us,
Jesus died, Jesus cared,
We're His bride, we're in heaven,
In the place He's prepared.

*Revelation 21:4 (NKJV)*
*And God will wipe away every tear from their eyes;*
*there shall be no more death, nor sorrow, nor crying.*
*There shall be no more pain, for the former things have passed away.*

Composed June 17, 2001

# How Sweet it Is

How sweet it is to have riches and fame,
Along with prestige and a popular name,
To enjoy the good life of parties and fun,
But what will you have when all of that's done?

When all the loud music and madness is past,
And you find out the happiness just did not last,
And after the flashing lights flicker and die
You'll discover you fell for the devil's big lie.

What a great price to pay; just consider the cost
When you say no to God, your soul you have lost.
Satan said he'd satisfy your every need,
But he's very deceitful, and clever indeed.

We will all have to stand before Jesus one day,
Tell me what will you hear the Blessed Lord say?
"Welcome home dear child, you've been faithful and true."
Or "Depart from Me sinner – I never knew you."

*2 Peter 2:9 (NKJV)*
*... then the Lord knows how to deliver the godly out of temptations*
*and to reserve the unjust under punishment for the day of judgment ...*

Composed October 7, 2000

# Precious Moment

How very precious was that moment
When first he saw His lovely face,
His pain and suffering all ended,
He finished well the arduous race.

He's face to face with his redeemer,
See Jesus take him to His breast,
So tenderly He softly whispers,
"It's over son, now rest."

*Romans 13:12 (KJV)*
*The night is far spent, the day is at hand:*
*let us therefore cast off the works of darkness,*
*and let us put on the amour of light.*

Composed December 20, 2004

# The Lion and The Lamb

The world's systems are collapsing,
The foundations are crumbling fast;
Only what's built on the Solid Rock
Will endure and forever will last.

The nations look for a savior,
The false Christ will swiftly arise,
For those who are looking for Jesus,
He will suddenly break through the skies.

Caught up in a flash in a moment,
Will rise at the last trumpet sound,
People who refused or neglected His gift,
Are bewildered and left on the ground.

After the Great Tribulation-
One thousand years of peace;
A millennium free from evil and fear,
Strife, wars and famines will cease.

The Lord's prayer will then be answered,
He will reign the eternal "I AM"
His kingdom will come, His will will be done,
And the lion will lie with the lamb.

*Isaiah 11:6 (NKJV)*
*"The wolf also shall*
*dwell with the lamb,*
*The leopard shall lie down*
*with the young goat,*
*The calf and the young lion*
*and the fatling together;*
*And a little child*
*shall lead them.*

Composed April 29, 2003
# The Veil

How thin is the veil we pass through
As we pass from this life to another,
How hard to lose a loved one,
A mother, a father or brother.

Life is a vapor, Very brief so we're told
"Grab all the gusto, before you're too old,"
But soon all too soon
We all will lie lifeless and cold.

If you're saved, it is just the beginning,
For when you arrive on heaven's shore,
You'll meet Jesus and all of your loved ones
Who have died and gone on before.

So now, while your heart is still beating,
Get saved today without fail,
You don't know when Jesus will call you –
We all will pass through the veil.

*Hebrews 6:19 (NKJV)*
*This hope we have as an anchor of the soul, both sure and steadfast,*
*and which enters the Presence behind the veil.*

Composed April 22, 1997

# Under The Fig Tree

The winds of hell blew so very hard,
Would she at last capsize?
Weary in soul and body,
No one would hear her cries.

Alone she stood in the corner,
Sobbing she cried so hard,
So long she had given her very best,
Her heart so wounded and scarred.

And then in a blissful moment,
She was in a beautiful place,
Surrounded by flowers and velvety grass,
A realm without time and space.

A lovely, soft waterfall cascaded down,
This place, for her He had made,
His strong arms around her together they sat,
Alone in this beautiful glade.

*Revelation 21:7 (NKJV)*
*He who overcomes shall inherit all things,*
*and I will be his God and he shall be My son.*

Composed June 26, 2005

# The Worth of My Soul

I would learn the intrinsic worth of my soul,
It's hard to conceive what You've done,
Only You know the worth of my eternal soul,
You sacrificed Jesus Your Son.

Eternal life, I cannot attain it,
This gift from You to me,
If I refuse or neglect Your gift,
I'll be lost for eternity.

By faith I choose to believe it
And until we are face to face,
With my whole heart I thank You my Father
For Your love and amazing grace.

As the eons in heaven roll on and on
And hell's fires continue to burn,
I will learn the worth of my eternal soul,
It is then, only then will I learn.

*Psalm 56:13 (NKJV)*
*For You have delivered my soul from death.*
*Have You not kept my feet from falling,*
*That I may walk before God In the light of the living?*

# Time

It's nice to please your neighbors,
To have good health and fame;
It's great to be important,
To have a well-known name.

But time, it flies so swiftly,
We all are born to die;
It may be years I have to live,
Or maybe death is nigh.

This then is most important,
When I'm laid beneath the sod;
That my sins are all forgiven,
That my soul is right with God.

Time ends but we'll be living,
On and on in either place;
Take a moment, I implore you;
Don't neglect God's saving grace.

*Proverbs 27:1 (NKJV)*
*Do not boast about tomorrow,*
*For you do not know what a day may bring forth.*

# When Jesus Comes Back

When Jesus comes back to receive us,
We'll be gone in a moment in time;
Never more to be tempted by Satan,
Taken out of this world filled with crime.

I may have a cake in the oven,
I may have a dress half-sewed,
I may be washing the dishes,
Or driving our car down the road.

We'll be gone in a flash, in a moment,
Taken out of the place where we toiled;
No more pain, no more tears, no more heartache,
Never more will our garment be soiled.

What a hope, what a promise to cling to,
But how solemn to be left behind;
With no hope of eternal salvation,
Only trouble and wrath they did find.

*1 Thessalonians 4:16-18 (KJV)*
*For the Lord himself descend from heaven with a shout, with the voice*
*of the archangel, and with the trump of God: and the dead in Christ shall rise first:*
*Then we which are alive and remain shall be caught up together with them*
*in the clouds, to meet the Lord in the air; and so shall we ever be with the Lord.*
*Wherefore comfort one another with these words.*

## Too Late

He will step out of heaven
Into a beautiful cloud,
A great trumpet will sound
Through the earth clear and loud.

Graves will burst open,
The dead in Christ will arise.
When you hear the trumpet,
Will you also rise?

Fear grips your heart,
You realize you were wrong.
Now you search for a Bible
And think, "I waited too long."

The King of Kings had returned
To rapture His bride.
Together, forever
To be by His side.

At last the clouds drift away,
You stare into the blue,
He came-you weren't ready;
Now it's too late for you.

*Matthew 24:44 (KJV)*
*"Therefore be ye ready;*
*for in such an hour as ye think not*
*the Son of Man cometh."*

Composed March 12, 1997

# Your Turn

After every speech has been made,
After every trophy's been won,
After all of the laughing has died,
After all your work is done.

After all the wars have been fought,
And every song has been sung,
After all of your tears have been shed,
After all of the bells have rung.

After all of the roses have died
And the sun forever has set,
When the clock strikes the last time,
And you've paid your very last debt.

It is your turn to stand before God –
Will your good works you offer remain?
If you gained the whole world but lose your soul,
What, what have you gained?

He offered His Son in your place,
And you offer Him your filthy rags,
In place of the gift that He offers you
He turns from your gift and gags.

The angels escort you away,
Forever cast out of your sight,
To enter eternity helpless, alone,
Forever in blackness of night.

*Revelation 20:15 (NKJV)*
*And anyone not found*
*written in the Book of Life*
*was cast into the lake of fire.*

# CHAPTER 6
# EVANGELISM

## Go

Everywhere, everywhere, there are people in need;
People in bondage who cry to be freed;
Many are lonely with minds filled with fear,
They need to know that the Savior is near.

He longs to give them His wonderful peace;
For only in Him can they find full release.
He would forgive all their guilt and their sin,
And His own Spirit would flow from within.

May we who know Jesus as Savior and Friend,
Continue His work with a heart that will lend,
For we have the secret to set the world free,
The great commission is for you and for me.

*Matthew 28:19 (NASB95)*
*Go therefore and make disciples of all the nations,*
*baptizing them in the name of the Father and the Son and the Holy Spirit.*

Composed June 21, 2000

# Come Apart

He came when I was laid aside,
While in the stillness there,
As I opened up my heart to Him,
His presence filled the air.

Nothing really changed at all
But my Shepherd drew me near;
"He is enough!" I say to you
In this world so filled with fear.

The uncertainty I had was gone,
It melted like the snow,
And in its place a glorious peace –
He is enough, I know.

"In quiet and in confidence
Will be your strength," I heard,
He gently reassures me
By His spirit and His Word.

You may not know His plan for you,
He bids you "Come apart,"
Stay there, with Him until you know
He's been yearning for your heart.

*Zephaniah 3:17 (KJV)*
*He will quiet you with his love.*

Composed August 1, 2000

# If They Only Knew

The Shepherd had a little lamb
Whose heart was white as snow,
And everywhere the Shepherd went
The lamb was sure to go.

He led in pastures lush and green
By waters sparkling bright.
The lamb would nuzzle up to Him
Throughout the day and night.

One day he wandered from the flock
Far from the precious fold,
He came upon some other sheep,
Abandoned, weak and cold.

They told him of their troubles,
Of their fears and deep distress.
The little lamb simply replied,
"My Shepherd gives me rest."

"You don't belong here in this mess
Eating garbage from a heap.
Please come with me, no need to fear,
My Shepherd loves His sheep."

"He'll take you and He'll feed you –
Oh if you only knew,
But you must taste yourself and see;
New life He'll give to you."

"Aren't you hungry for sheep food?
There is plenty, come and see."
But through sad eyes and fearful hearts
They say, don't bother me.

"This is how it's always been,
We'll stay here 'til we die,
And little lamb began to see
They were blinded by a lie.

The Shepherd soon came seeking,
It was raining, dark and cold,
And with strong arms He carried him back
To the safety of the fold.

"I am so glad to be back home,
I am so safe with you,"
But tears of sadness filled his eyes –
"Oh if they only knew."

*John 10:11 (KJV)*
*I am the good shepherd:*
*the good shepherd giveth his life*
*for the sheep.*

"Christ Jesus came into the world to save sinners"

# FAMILY

Composed April 2014

## Better Than Gold

"Close your eyes,
Open your hands."
I did just what he said,
As I opened my eyes I saw
A book that had been read.

It was not new, but beautiful,
I was grateful beyond measure,
Often when I read the words
I find-
He has given me a treasure.

I love my precious grandson
He's very handsome, tall and smart,
But this book my grandson gave me
Was given from his heart.

*Romans 14:19 (NKJV)*

*Therefore, let us pursue the things which make for peace and the things by which one may edify another.*

Composed April 27, 2004

# One Drop

"How long is eternity, Grandpa?"
A boy inquired one day,
The old man thought for a while,
Then together they made their way.

They soon stood on a sandy beach,
And as far as their eyes could see
Were miles and miles of water.
Was this as big as eternity?

Grandpa had taken an eyedropper,
Bending down, he filled it up,
His grandson did not understand
Why he put just one drop in the cup.

"Son, this one drop is what we call time,
Eternity has no end,"
The young boy tried to grasp it,
It was so hard to comprehend.

"We'll meet Jesus and all of the others
Who have died and gone on before,
I think they're now waiting for us
To arrive on heaven's shore."

"Eternity sure will be long, grandpa,"
Nudging closer to his grandpa's knee,
As the sun set over the water,
Creating a golden sea.

*Psalm 121:8 (NKJV)*
*The LORD shall preserve your going out and your coming in*
*from this time forth, and even forevermore.*

Composed June 5, 2000

# Wedding Day

Wedding day coming.
Excitement mounting,
When in great anticipation
The Father gives the bride away.

# Mothers

The powerful influence of a mother,
The model of her example is strong,
Whether good or bad she is forming a life,
Lingering with us all our life long.

Composed September 20, 2003

# My Mother

Remembering my mother,
I cannot help but see,
Those work worn hands that toiled long
From dawn til' dusk for me.

Remembering my mother,
Her unselfish tender love,
Were truly characteristic of
The One she loved above.

Remembering my mother,
I don't think of her as dead;
She's in heaven rejoicing,
She followed Jesus where He led.

The arms that held me,
The hands that fed me,
Are buried so deep
Beneath the sod.

Her love that taught me, her frown that scolded me,
Her voice that encouraged me to go on.
Are silent forever, separation is painful
But she is at rest at home with God.

I wish I had one more chance, Lord,
To talk to my mother once more,
But I'll talk to her when we're together,
Over yonder, on heaven's bright shore.

*Proverbs 22:6 (KJV)*
*Train up a child in a way he should go*
*and when he is old, he will not depart from it.*

# FORGIVENESS

Composed July 21, 2010

## Abundant Pardon

More than anything in daily life
If what I say or do,
Disappoints my Lord and Savior
It grieves me through and through.

I must turn back, confess to Him,
And when I meet Him in the garden,
Once again, I'm overwhelmed
And receive abundant pardon.

*Isaiah 55:7 (KJV)*
*"Let the wicked forsake his way, and the unrighteous man his thoughts:*
*and let him return unto the Lord, and he will have mercy upon him;*
*and to our God, for he will abundantly pardon."*

# No Other Way

Did You really have to suffer,
Did you really have to die?
So that we might be forgiven
And someday live with You on high?

Wasn't there some other way, Lord?
You made such a sacrifice;
It's far beyond my comprehension,
To think you paid so great a price.

So many questions, we may ponder,
While living here on earth below.
So like a child we simply trust Him;
The answers we may never know.

Yes, long before creation started,
He knew that dreadful day would come
When cruel men would vent their hatred.
Yet still, He knew there would be some
Who would believe and seek to serve him,
Who would worship and obey.
And so, He gave himself a ransom
Because there was no other way.

*Hebrews 9:22 (KJV)*
*And without shedding of blood is no remission*

# GLORY

Composed October 1, 2000

## Everything

Everything beautiful, everything grand,
Everything we hold fast in this great land,
Good music, the arts, every beautiful day,
Will soon be gone, this will all pass away.

The stars in the heavens, so wondrous and fair,
The trees in the forest and the birds in the air,
The cities we built, so mighty and strong,
Nothing remaineth, not even a song.

I turn to the Bible, so steadfast and sure,
And read that His Word will forever endure,
It will stand ere the oceans are silent for aye;
It is settled in heaven, it will not pass away.

Lord, Your Holy Spirit You have given to me;
He comforts and helps me His glory to see.
What else could I ask for, I need nothing more,
Until I am safe on that heavenly shore.

So help me, dear Father, as I seek to serve Thee,
To read Your Word daily, it's so precious to me.
This world is decaying and soon will be past,
I resolve to stand firm on the things that will last.

*Hebrews 1:12 (NIV)*
*You will roll them up like a robe; like a garment they will be changed.*
*But you remain the same, and your years will never end."*

Composed October 6, 2004

# Moments of Glory

Waiting in His presence
The Holy Spirit very still,
He only knows my heart beats
To do God's perfect will.

A wordless conversation
No words could ever say,
The glory in these moments
Love melts the words away.

*Psalm 37:7 (KJV)*
*Rest in the Lord, and wait patiently for him: fret not thyself because of him who prospereth in his way, because of the man who bringeth wicked devices to pass.*

# Oh, the Glory!

Fountains of the deep are now breaking open,
Great rivers are gushing forth,
Springs of worship at last spilling over,
Living water is filling the earth.

Oceans of tears are filling His bottles,
His glory is being revealed,
The bride of Christ is being perfected
As she submits to His Lordship and yields.

*John 11:40 (NASB95)*
*Jesus said to her,*
*"Did I not say to you that if you believe,*
*you will see the glory of God?"*

Composed August 29, 2000

# Your Bride

So very precious to Your heart,
Your precious bride,
Your precious bride.

For her You shed Your blood and died,
Your precious bride,
Your precious bride.

Not everyone who hears will come,
Only Your bride,
Only your bride.

Forever with You, by Your side,
Your precious bride,
Your precious bride.

*Revelation 19:9 (NIV)*
*Then the angel said to me, "Write this: Blessed are those*
*who are invited to the wedding supper of the Lamb!"*
*And he added, "These are the true words of God."*

# CHAPTER 7

# GOD'S WORD

## A Conqueror's Crown

Put on the full armor
Do not take it off;
You must never give in
Or even get soft.

Every demon of hell
Is under your feet,
Soldier of God
You will not know defeat.

Empowered by His Spirit
His Word going forth,
Speak to the East, West,
South and the North,

"Be free in the mighty
Name of the Lord"
Stand firm in His righteousness
And pick up His Sword."

Your weapons are mighty
To pull strongholds down,
Fight on and He'll give you
A conqueror's crown.

*Ephesians 6:11 (KJV)*
*Put on the whole armor of God,*
*that ye may be able to stand*
*against the wiles of the devil.*

# Be Still and Know

The words "silent" and "listen" have the same letters,
I learned from my grandson one day,
"How very interesting, " I said, and pondered it through the day.
Then finding the verse, and reading the words very slow,
How very needful it is for me every day to take time to
"Be still and know."

*Psalm 46:10 (NKJV)*
*Be still, and know that I am God;*
*I will be exalted among the nations,*
*I will be exalted in the earth!*

Composed May 21, 2000

# It Pays to Serve Jesus

It pays to serve Jesus completely,
I'd hear Christians say now and then;
I wondered if they were just talking,
For never had I been born again.

I would read the words in the Bible,
And they sounded good in my ears;
But I truly didn't believe them,
I doubted and even had fears.

But then one beautiful evening,
The Spirit came over my soul;
He gave me great peace like a river,
He made me complete, now I'm whole.

Those promises there in the Bible
Are true and I'm learning each day;,
To trust even more in the Savior,
I have found that it truly does pay.

*2 Peter 1:4 (KJV)*
*Whereby are given unto us exceeding great and precious promises:*
*that by these ye might be partakers of the divine nature,*
*having escaped the corruption that is in the world through lust.*

Composed February 12, 2008

# Know Him

The way to get to know Him
In this world of sin and strife,
Is to slowly read the Word of God,
Digest the Bread of Life.

You will see and know what love is –
Your eyes will open wide,
See Jesus in the scriptures,
He is Love personified.

*Romans 5:8 (KJV)*
*But God commendeth his love toward us, in that,*
*while we yet sinners, Christ died for us.*

Composed March 10, 2004

# O God, Early will I Seek Thee

I have nothing to give when I'm empty and dry.
I must receive from Him,
I must go to the well and meet Him there
And be filled again to the brim.

When I leave the well refreshed and renewed,
Prepared to face another day,
Someone may catch the overflow
I may spill along the way.

*Psalm 63:1 (KJV)*
*O God, thou art my God; early will I seek thee: my soul thirsteth for thee, my flesh*
*longeth for thee in a dry and thirsty land, where no water is;*

# My Bible

I own a book, a precious book,
The Author is divine.
It has truths that I may gather,
Written deep in every line.

There are some people in the masses
In some far and distant lands,
Who will never see a Bible,
Will never hold one in their hands.

How they long to see this treasure,
They would gladly suffer pain;
For one page in their possession,
They take the risk of being slain.

I thank you, Jesus, for my Bible,
I will try to read it every day.
For it truly is a privilege
To read Your Word each day and pray.

**Hebrews 4:12 (KJV)**

*For the word of God is quick, and powerful, and sharper than any two-edged sword,*
*piercing even to the dividing asunder of soul and spirit, and the joints and marrow,*
*and is the discerner of thoughts and intents of the heart.*

Composed January 23, 1995

## Crystal Clear Water

I want to be where the rivers are flowing,
Where the waters run crystal clear;
I am longing to hear Your still small voice
And feel Your presence near.

I detest the drink the world would give;
The waters are polluted with sin,
Only the streams that flow from You
Satisfy my spirit within.

Nothing or no one can take Your place;
You alone are my joy and delight.
Holy Spirit please come and reveal Him to me
I ask in His name tonight.

*1 Corinthians 2:10-16 (KJV)*
*But God hath revealed them*
*unto us by his Spirit:*
*for the Spirit searcheth all things,*
*yea, the deep things of God.*

Composed November 18, 2002

# Give Us Revelation

Oh give to us the revelation,
We are so precious in Your sight,
May we know Your tender mercy,
Drench us in Your holy light.

It is when we see You only,
It is then the dawn will come,
The long, dark night is finally over,
The Son is rising, Life has come.

*Matthew 17:8 (KJV)*
*And when they had lifted up their eyes,*
*they saw no man, save Jesus only.*

Composed May 7, 2006

# Wash Me

Lord Jesus, I am sorry,
I hate the tinge of sin,
Wash me, wash me in your blood –
Make me clean within.

Cause me to turn from folly,
To not say things that grieve,
I would be a healing stream,
While I live and breathe.

*Ephesians 4:29 (NIV)*
*Do not let any unwholesome talk come out of your mouths, but only what is helpful*
*for building others up according to their needs, that it may benefit those who listen.*

## Days of Grace

The leaves are falling,
The skies are growing dark,
Harsh winds are beginning to blow,
And winter's about to embark.

The days of grace are flying by fast
Signs of the end are here.

What a glorious and grand proclamation

The coming of the Lord is near.
The coming of the Lord is near.

**Titus 3:7 (KJV)**
*That being justified by his grace, we should be made heirs*
*according to the hope of eternal life.*

# Words

Are all of the words you say
Seasoned with salt?
Do they lift and encourage the heart?
Or do they at times inflict
Heartache and pain,
Like a swift, sharp flying dart?

Words fitly spoken
Can bring gladness and joy;
Let your speech be always with grace,
Let them bring comfort,
Forgiveness and life,
To everyone, every time, every place.

**Colossians 4:6 (KJV)**
*Let your speech always be with grace, seasoned with salt,
that you may know how you ought to answer each one.*

# HEART

Composed May 31, 2007

## Heart Beat

What makes your heart beat faster?
What really lights up your fire?
What is your top priority?
What is your heart's desire?

*Matthew 22:37 (KJV)*
*Jesus said unto him, "Thou shalt love the Lord thy God with all thy heart,*
*and with all thy soul, and with all thy mind."*

Composed March 1, 1996

## Heart's Desire

You alone
Are my heart's desire
And I long to worship Thee.

You alone
Are my strength and shield,
To You alone
Does my spirit yield.

*Psalm 42:1 (KJV)*
*As the deer pants for water. so my soul panteth after thee, O God.*

Composed February 12, 2001

# To Mend a Heart

When Jesus said I love you,
He stretched His arms out wide,
He willingly was put to death,
For Love was crucified.

Agape love is costly,
It demands a sacrifice.
It's far, far more than wedding bells,
Old shoes, a bag of rice.

For when you say, 'I love you,'
And still have selfishness and pride,
You really do not love at all,
'Till all your "self" has died.

In giving all you then receive,
This is what God intended;
To live you must decide to die,
Then will your heart be mended.

*Matthew 22:37 (NKJV)*
*Jesus said to him, "You shall love the LORD your God*
*with all your heart, with all your soul, and with all your mind."*

Composed May 29, 1997

# Matters of The Heart

In the matters of my heart,
He ponders hard and long,
He longs for me to trust and know
His love for me, so strong.

I am the apple of His eye,
When I choose to disobey
I cause Him grief and sorrow
In a Father kind of way.

This is the way, walk in it,
Though you may not understand,
This is the way My child,
Keep holding to My hand.

It is only in obedience,
Though His love I cannot earn,
The matters of my heart reveal,
I love Him in return.

*Psalm 13:5 (KJV)*
*But I have trusted in thy mercy; my heart shall rejoice in thy salvation.*

Composed November 4, 2006

# Not for Fame

Not for fame or riches
Does my heart aspire,
To capture
What has captured me
To my one desire.

*Psalm 51:10 (KJV)*
*Create in me a clean heart, O God; and renew a right spirit within me.*

Composed November 19, 1996

# Tears

Thinking of You,
Your presence so real,
My heart overflows
Through my eyes as I kneel,
Tears of pain, tears of joy,
Tears of deep gratitude,
Tears of grief and compassion
For the vast multitude.

*Revelation 21:4 (NKJV)*
*And God will wipe away every tear from their eyes;*
*there shall be no more death, nor sorrow, nor crying.*
*There shall be no more pain,*
*for the former things have passed away.*

# CHAPTER 8

# JESUS CHRIST

Composed September 1, 2005

## A Giver, A Taker

A woman poured her ointment
On Jesus' precious head,
His disciples became indignant,
"It was a waste," they said.

Judas told the high priest,
"I'll do it for a fee,
I'll deliver Jesus unto you;
What will you give to me?"

*Matthew 26:14, 15 (KJV)*

*Then ... Judas Iscariot, went unto the chief priests and said unto them,*
*"What will ye give me and I will deliver Him unto you?"*
*And they covenanted with him for thirty pieces of silver.*

Composed January 21, 2003

## Great Is the Lord!

Awed by the glory of His loveliness,
Succumbed by the power of His might,
Overtaken by waves of His love divine,
Consumed in the beauty of His light.

Wrapped in a blanket of billowy clouds,
Dancing from star to star,
Finding His love is infinity,
Much greater than imagined by far.

*Matthew 17:2 (KJV)*

*And He was transfigured before them:*
*and His face did shine as the sun, and His raiment was white as the light.*

Composed November 7.2010

# Angels

Angels announced to the shepherds
Jesus' glorious birth,
And angels appeared to the disciples
When He ascended the earth.

Soon the archangel will shout –
It will be heard clear and loud;
Jesus Himself will descend
From heaven in a cloud.

*Acts 1:11 (NKJV)*
*"Men of Galilee, why do you stand gazing up into heaven?*
*This same Jesus, who was taken up from you into heaven,*
*will so come in like manner as you saw Him go into heaven."*

# Emmanuel
*(God With Us)*

My God, my God, in human form
I cannot understand,
In power and great humbleness
He walked the sea and land.

I see Him in a manger
In swaddling clothes upon the straw,
I look at His surroundings;
The filth within this animal stall.

I see Him eat and drink with sinners,
He laid His majesty aside.
I see His Love, His deep compassion
So free of selfishness and pride.

I see Him with little children,
He gently smooths their tousled hair,
"What kind of man?" the people marvel
To see Him with children there.

Then kneeling down to His disciples
I see the magnitude of grace,
He girds Himself, then with a towel
I see Him take the servant's place.

I see Him beaten, torn asunder,
I see the love He had for me,
The God of all creation dying;
My Lord, my God how can it be?

But He arose, victorious Conqueror,
Heaven and all creation sings,
And very soon in joy and splendor
I'll see Him crowned "King of Kings."

*Philippians 2:7 (KJV)*
*But made himself of no reputation,*
*and took upon him the form of a servant,*
*and was made in the likeness of men:*

Composed May 6, 2008

# The Pearl of Great Price

If you seek Him with your whole heart,
There will be a price to pay,
But let nothing or no one detain you,
Allow nothing to stand in your way.

Surrender your life and die to self
As a living sacrifice,
Seek until you find Him,
He is the pearl of great price.

*Matthew 13:43 & 46 (KJV)*
*Then shall the righteous shine forth as the sun in the kingdom of their Father.*
*Who hath ears to hear, let him hear. Who, when he had found one pearl*
*of great price, went and sold all that he had, and bought it.*

# He Draws Me

Walking with Jesus day after day,
Seeing His glory as I worship and pray;
No words can express all the joy that I feel,
His sweet Holy Spirit is so vibrant and real.

There are times I'm not willing to really press in,
Or I may wander off and be tempted by sin,
But soon, very soon, I'm so empty and dry,
I must find my way back or I'll wither and die.

I stray but He draws me
Back to His side;
Only with Jesus
Can I be satisfied.

*John 7:38 (KJV)*
*"He who believes in Me, as the Scripture said,*
*'From his innermost being will flow rivers of living water.'"*

# How Big?

A child may ask, "How big is God?"
But I often wonder too,
When I gaze into a starry sky
Or at an ocean blue.

He makes each flower in the field,
And He tames the angry sea;
He knows each child in Asia,
Still, He has His eye on me.

He takes the time to listen
To each and every prayer.
No matter where I go today,
His love is everywhere.

He desires that I worship
And call Him Father when we pray;
He longs for me to know Him,
In a deep and intimate way.

How big is God? I wonder,
But in my finite mind;
I'll never comprehend His love,
The words I cannot find.

So, in growing adoration,
From an overflowing heart,
I cannot help but say to Him,
My God, How Great Thou Art!

*Luke 9:43 (NKJV)*
*And they were all amazed at the greatness of God. But while everyone was*
*marveling at all that He was doing, He said to His disciple.*

# I AM

Walking on the narrow pathway,
Spotless snow-white little lamb,
Joyful in her Shepherd's keeping,
She follows close, the Great "I AM"

A roaring lion's on the prowl –
He knows the lamb is almost home,
Watching waiting for that moment,
If this lamb decides to roam.

Oh, you must stay close,
Stay close little lamb,
Stay close to your Shepherd,
The almighty "I AM."

*John 8:58 (KJV)*
*Jesus said unto them, Verily, verily, I say unto you,*
*"Before Abraham was, I AM."*

# Only Jesus

Completely fulfilled in the spirit,
Possessing the joy that He brings,
Knowing at dusk and at daybreak
I'm under His almighty wings.

He is here every moment I sense Him,
All else is nauseous and wrong,
A stranger, a foreigner, a pilgrim
In this world I no longer belong.

*Psalm 91:4 (NKJV)*
*He shall cover you with His feathers,*
*and under His wings you shall take refuge;*
*His truth shall be your shield and buckler.*

# Jesus

There are no words except to say
He is "Wonderful" in every way;
He is the all wise "Counselor"
So patient, kind and good,
How sad by countless millions
He is so misunderstood.

"The Mighty God" yes "Mighty God"
I am in awe of You;
The grandeur of the universe
And early morning dew.

"The Everlasting Father"
Always watching over me;
There is no one here, on earth below
That would compare with Thee.

You are the ruler of my heart,
You cause the storms to cease,
In all of life's uncertainties
You are "The Prince of Peace."

*Isaiah 9:6 (NKJV)*
*For unto us a Child is born, unto us a Son is given;*
*And the government will be upon His shoulder.*
*And His name will be called*
*Wonderful, Counselor, Mighty God,*
*Everlasting Father, Prince of Peace.*

# My Savior

Walking ever nearer
To my precious Lord and King,
I'm rejoicing in His sunshine
As He gives me songs to sing.

Yesterday, I loved Him dearly,
Still today I love Him more,
And I know that on that morrow
He'll be sweeter than before.

The Holy Spirit lives within,
Makes Jesus real to me;
Like the blooming of a lovely spring,
His loveliness I see.

I thank Thee, O dear Father,
I will forever be,
In love with Christ my Savior,
Who bled and died for me.

**1 John 1:7 (NASB95)**
*but if we walk in the Light as He Himself is in the Light, we have fellowship with one another, and the blood of Jesus His Son cleanses us from all sin.*

Jesus Christ 129

# Portrait of Love

Down through the long dark corridors
He came to earth below
To demonstrate His love for us
He wanted us to know.

Born in the town of Bethlehem,
Wise men came from afar,
They found Him there in a manger,
Led by a beautiful star.

He grew in stature and wisdom,
Did many miraculous things;
They watched Him in awe and amazement;
Life, hope and gladness He brings.

The children came running to Jesus
To Him they were never a bother,
As they playfully gathered around Him
They were seeing their heavenly Father.

He healed the sick and raised up the dead,
Calmed the wild and stormy sea,
Multiplied the loaves and fishes,
Set a wild possessed man free.

He opened up the languid eyes
Of a man who was born blind,
In Cana, at the wedding feast,
He turned water into wine.

They hated Him without cause,
They cried, "Crucify this man!"
They would not stop until they saw
His blood streaming in the sand.

They nailed Him to a Roman cross,
Suspended in midair,
The God of all creation
"Sitting down they watched Him there."

The images of almighty God,
Left glory and splendor above,
His life – His death so clearly revealed –
A beautiful portrait of love.

*John 10:37, 38 (NASB95)*
*"If I do not do the works of My Father, do not believe Me; but if I do them, though you do not believe Me, believe the works, so that you may know and understand that the Father is in Me, and I in the Father."*

## Spices

They came and brought You spices
When You were newly born,
Then when You were crucified
They brought spices the next morn.

I too would bring You spices;
Gold, frankincense and myrrh.
Is this what You desire from me?
What gift would You prefer?

I read You search throughout the earth
For one to lift their voice,
Who worships You in spirit,
This should cause You to rejoice.

How wonderful this gift of Love;
Yourself, a sacrifice.
May the worship from my grateful heart,
Be as a fragrant spice.

*John 12:3 (KJV)*

*Then Mary took a pound of very costly oil of spikenard,*
*anointed the feet of Jesus, and wiped His feet with her hair.*
*And the house was filled with the fragrance of the oil.*

# Stop, Look and Listen

Won't you stop for just a moment,
You need to stop and fix your gaze;
See from His head, the blood and spittle,
The crowd inflicted in their rage.

Listen to the steady pounding,
As the nails are pierced into His hands;
He's lifted up, His blood is flowing,
Like a stream upon the sands.

Now listen to the words He utters,
While dying on the tree He made;
"Forgive them Father," cries the Savior,
As all our sins on Him were laid.

Go on your way now but remember,
This scene you saw, it was for you;
Today the question you must answer,
Do you believe He died for you?

*Luke 23:24 (KJV)*
*Then said Jesus, "Father, forgive them; for they know not what they do."*
*And they parted his raiment, and cast lots.*

# The Apple of His Eye

The "apple of His eye" are you,
So precious in His sight;
How tenderly He cherishes
And guards you through the night.

How beautiful to realize,
In a very finite measure;
That you are, oh, so dear to Him,
You are His greatest treasure.

A beautiful endearment,
How very tender is the eye.
So it must hurt the Father,
When He sees His child cry.

He loves you and He understands,
When you doubt and ask Him, "Why?"
But let Him tenderly embrace you,
You're the "apple of His eye."

*Matthew 17:8 (KJV)*

*Keep me as the apple of the eye, hide me under the shadow of thine wings*

Composed December 2012

# This Turbulent Age

They arrived in Bethlehem
So weary from it all,
Mary, at last brought forth her child
Inside an animal stall.

As she watched Him grow,
She pondered,
And she knew this from the start,
He was unlike the other boys,
He was kind and pure in heart.

The days and years swiftly flew by
Since He slept upon her breast.
One day she marveled when He said,
"Come unto Me and rest."

His words are still alive today,
They are written on the page.
He speaks to us who are living today
In this present turbulent age.

*Matthew 11:28-30 (KJV)*
*Come unto me, all ye that labor and are heavy laden, and I will give you rest.*
*Take my yoke upon you, and learn of me; for I am meek and lowly in heart;*
*and ye shall find rest unto your souls. For my yoke is easy, and my burden is light.*

## A Love Bath

Do you hurt deep in your spirit,
And no one seems to understand?
Do you feel alone, forsaken,
In a dry and weary land?

God is love, He wants to heal you,
But you must let all feelings die,
Then His love will come and feel you,
And yes, He has a vast supply.

Jesus has a large, soft love sponge,
A bottle full of balm,
He'll bathe you in His love and mercy
And leave you clean, refreshed and calm.

Then He'll bring a lovely blanket,
And gently wrap you all around,
And when you feel His love surround you,
You will be free, no longer bound.

*1 John 4:18 (KJV)*
*There is no fear in love;*
*but perfect love casteth out fear;*
*because fear hath torment.*
*He that feareth is not made in perfect love.*

Composed November 10, 2003

# A Wrap

"You need a wrap it's cold out there,"
Remember calling out to your son,
He'd run back in and grab a coat,
So full of energy and fun.

Before you feel the chill of this world,
And before you begin your day,
"Come away" and "be still," and meet with God,
Before you go on your way.

Sit by a window and ponder His love,
As the sun begins to rise,
His mercy is new every morning,
His faithfulness to the skies.

Before you begin your work for the day,
Meet with your Father above,
As His child, you need reassurance,
Let Him wrap you again in His love.

*Psalm 91:14 (KJV)*
*Because he hath set his love upon me,*
*therefore will I deliver him:*
*I will set him on high,*
*because he hath known my name.*

## All or Nothing

You do not begin to know His love,
The Creator of all you see;
Your mind can't know the depths of His love –
Your spirit man must see.

You've tried to understand His love,
You feel it's been concealed;
But it's not in understanding
His love must be revealed.

Surrender, give Him all of your heart,
This is the place you must start,
He does not accept or deserve lukewarm –
You must love Him with all your heart.

*Mark 12:30 (KJV)*
*And thou shalt love the Lord thy God*
*with all thy heart, and with all thy soul,*
*and with all thy mind, and with all thy strength:*
*this is the first commandment.*

Composed January 4, 2001

# Christ's Image

Enveloped in a life-giving capsule,
Swimming in love so divine,
An intimate, most beautiful place that's so holy,
With great reverence and freedom combined.

Completely engulfed in His warm tender Spirit
He broods as a sweet gentle dove,
Unseen revelations disclosing His beauty,
Completely dependent, knowing His love.

Enveloped, engulfed as a babe in the womb,
His soft voice and heartbeat I know,
Constant abiding, becoming like Jesus,
As into Christ's image I grow.

**John 15:9 (KJV)**
*As the Father hath loved me, so have I loved you: continue ye in my love.*

Composed October 20, 1999

## Jesus' Love

When I read of His love in the Bible,
It touches my heart every time;
It's beyond any human emotion,
And to think that this Savior is mine.

His love has been put to music,
When it's sung, I am thrilled through and through,
When alone, I can sing and it lifts me,
Praise the Lord, He makes everything new.

I can see His love working through people,
In their words and actions so kind,
It brings me great joy and real blessing,
But this love is not easy to find.

I'm thankful for friends who know Jesus,
Who have helped me through laughter and tears,
And this love that has bound us together
Will abide until Jesus appears.

*Ephesians 3:19 (KJV)*
*And to know the love of Christ, which passeth knowledge,*
*that ye might be filled with all the fulness of God.*

Composed February 9, 2003

# Know His Love

You do not begin to know His love,
The Creator of all you see,
But your mind cannot know the depths of His love
Your spirit man must see.

You've tried to understand His love,
You think it's been concealed,
But it is not in understanding
His love must be revealed.

Practice being His beloved child,
You're one of a kind you know,
Cry out to Him as a boy –
You're His son and He loves you so.

*1 John 4:16 (KJV)*
*And we have known and believed the love that God hath to us.*
*God is love; and he that dwelleth in love dwelleth in God, and God in him.*

Composed November 25, 2002

# Love Him Always

When the Spirit blows the fire is kindled –
Love Him then.
Do not wait A moment longer –
Love Him then.
Never, ever quench the Spirit,
Whisper softly, 'Lord I love You,'
When your tears
Are softly falling –
Love Him then.

*1 Thessalonians 5:19 (KJV)*
*Quench not the Spirit.*

# Martha

Martha's busy in the kitchen,
Busy cooking up a storm.
Special dishes. ironed linen,
Everything served fresh and warm.

"Jesus, eating at my table,
He is such a special guest.
I wonder if He's hungry,
I hope my biscuits pass the test."

"Mary's out there in the front room,
Seated there at Jesus' feet.
I wish she was a bit more helpful,
Make the salad or slice the meat."

"Martha, please come here for just a moment,
You need to stop and take a rest.
"I can't now Lord, I'm much too busy,
Besides – You deserve the best."

"Martha, Martha, I'd be happy
With some soup, a piece of bread.
You've worked so hard, but I desire
Your precious company instead.

*Luke 10:40 (NKJV)*
*But Martha was distracted*
*with much serving,*
*and she approached Him and said,*
*"Lord, do You not care that my sister*
*has left me to serve alone?*
*Therefore, tell her to help me."*

Composed May 8, 2001

# More of Him

I'm hiding in the crevice,
The crevice of the "Rock,"
His love is all around me,
And softens every shock.

I don't even fear the future,
"My Daddy" holds the key,
Deep within this shelter
He is taking care of me.

He showed me in the Inner man
How big He is, how big He is,
And oh my spirit leaped within,
He's full of love, so full of love.

I will never comprehend,
He died for me. He died for me,
Consumed within, and yearning still,
For more of Him, for more of Him.

*Romans 5:8 (KJV)*
*But God commended his love toward us, in that,*
*while we were yet sinners, Christ for us.*

Composed May 20, 1990

# Ocean of Mercy

I am bathed in an ocean of mercy,
I swim in deep waters of love,
I feel swift currents of power
Flowing straight from the Father above.

*Ezekiel 47:5 (KJV)*
*Afterward he measured a thousand; and it was a river that I could not pass over:*
*for the waters were risen, waters to swim in, a river that could not be passed over.*

Composed December 5, 2009

# Perfect Love

I saw His great love when on Calvary He died,
But to know His love – it is so deep and wide.
I'm in beautiful waters way over my head
Alive in His womb, to this world I am dead.
His fulfilling consummates every wish;
To know Him in spirit is glory and bliss.

*Romans 8:39 (NKJV)*
*... nor height nor depth, nor any other created thing,*
*shall be able to separate us from the love of God*
*which is in Christ Jesus our Lord.*

Composed May 12, 1998

# To the Bride

Oh, I will not forsake you
In your time of need.

I cannot deny myself
Your begotten of My Seed.

And all of life's disparagements
Can't hide you from My love.

I have betrothed you to My Son;
The wedding feast is soon begun.

For just a little while,
Hold fast until I come.

*Revelation 21:9 (NKJV)*
*Then one of the seven angels...came to me and talked with me, saying,*
*"Come, I will show you the bride, the Lamb's wife."*

Composed July 8, 2008
## Two Masters

Take a look at the two masters,
We all serve one of the two,
One is out to kill you –
The other One died for you.

Your eternal soul lies in the balance,
Who do you obey?
The answer is found deep in your heart –
Who do you love today?

**Matthew 6:24 (KJV)**
*"No man can serve two masters; For either he will hate the one, and love the other,*
*or else he will hold to the one, and despise the other."*

Composed September 15, 2004
## Your Love

Words have been written,
Songs have been sung,
But we've not even started,
We've not yet begun,

To tell of His greatness
His power and might,
We have failed in our efforts
Fallen short in our plight;

Lord, oh my God
You are glorious to me,
I will learn of Your love
Throughout eternity.

**Matthew 19:26 (KJV)**
*But Jesus beheld them, and said unto them, with men this is impossible;*
*but with God all things are possible.*

# CHAPTER 9

# NEGLECT

Composed July 14, 1996

## Depart

With words God made the universe,
He spoke, it came to be,
But inside my very being
He speaks so tenderly.

He set the mountains in their place,
Makes the mighty oceans roar,
But He waits for me to answer
Gently knocking on my door.

So powerful, so tender,
I do not understand,
As once again I ponder
The nail print in His hand.

He cried out loud on Calvary,
"They know not what they do,"
Unconditional agape love
He has for me and you.

Today He says, "Come unto me"
Men laugh and go their way,
They neglect so great salvation,
There will be a judgement day.

His final words, "Depart from Me"
Will strike terror to their heart,
No prayer, no tears will help them then,
When they hear His word, "Depart!"

*Matthew 25:41 (NKJV)*
*Then He will also say to those on the left hand, "Depart from Me, you cursed,*
*into the everlasting fire prepared for the devil and his angels."*

Composed May 4, 2003

# Neglect

There is no hope outside of Jesus,
There is no hope found for your soul.
You have no hope of eternal salvation
While the ages of eternity roll.

He came so far to save you,
God came all the way down for you.
You will have no excuse when you stand before God,
You'll have nothing to say or do.

You could have been saved forever,
But your name is not found in the book.
Neglect has cost you your eternal soul,
The Judge gives you one final look.

"I never knew you, take him away!"
His words pierce your heart like a knife,
You put it off once too often –
Get saved, while you still have life

*Mark 8:36 (KJV)*
*"For what shall it profit a man,*
*if he shall gain the whole world,*
*and lose his own soul?"*

# The Ark

Evil pressing in all over,
God's judging this abundant land,
Woe to those who do not know Him,
Who will not hold a nail-pierced hand.

It's coming fast, the clouds are gathering,
It's building fast and getting dark –
There is no place to run for refuge
Except to Jesus Christ "The Ark."

*Romans 2:3 (NKJV)*
*And do you think this, O man, you who judge those practicing such things,*
*and doing the same, that you will escape the judgment of God?*

Composed August 8, 2009

# Today's Multitude

Bold, rude and unruly,
A boisterous wild crowd,
Spiritually blind in deep darkness,
Listening to "rock" hard and loud.

Still today, God looks down from heaven,
And ponders their hearts cold and hard,
For this wicked and perverse generation,
He was beaten and unmercifully marred.

Their soul, their souls are so precious,
Worth more than mere words can tell,
He alone knows the worth of their eternal soul
He died to save them from hell.

*Hebrews 2:3 (NKJV)*
*How shall we escape if we neglect so great a salvation,*
*which at the first began to be spoken by the Lord,*
*and was confirmed to us by those who heard Him.*

# PEACE

## At Jesus' Feet

When your burden gets too heavy
And everything is black as night,
You need to stop and seek out Jesus,
Then everything will be alright.

There are times when friends can't help you,
They can't feel your aching heart;
Only Jesus knows your battle,
He alone can peace impart.

That old serpent's out to get you,
He tries to sift you out like wheat,
We need like Mary to be spending
Much more time at Jesus' feet.

Pour your heart out, He will listen,
And will gently ease your pain;
How refreshing is His spirit,
Falling down like gentle rain.

*Job 41:22 (KJV)*
*"Sorrow is turned into joy before him."*

Composed March 3, 1997

# Pain Removed

He released the sting
Within my heart
Sharp arrows had inflicted,
Satan's big intentions were
So cruel, mean and wicked.

Calling out to God my Father,
My efforts, all in vain;
Only He knew the method
To remove my deepest pain.

*Luke 4:18 (KJV)*

*The spirit of the Lord is upon me, because he hath anointed me to preach the gospel
to the poor; he hath sent me to heal the brokenhearted, to preach deliverance to the
captives, and recovering of sight to the blind, to set at liberty them that are bruised.*

Composed November 18, 2002

# Son is Rising

Oh, give to us the revelation,
We are so precious in Your sight,
May we know Your tender mercy,
Drench us in Your Holy Light.

It is when we see You only,
It is then the dawn will come,
The long, dark night is finally over,
The Son is rising, Life has come.

*Matthew 17:8 (KJV)*

*And when they had lifted up their eyes, they saw no man, save Jesus only.*

Composed July 8, 1998

# If

If you never saw a lovely red rose
And behold its glory so grand,
I could try to describe its beauty to you,
But you never would understand.

If you never tasted a tree-ripened peach
Only rain, sun and time can make,
You never would know the goodness therein,
Until you yourself would partake.

The rose we see and the fruit we must eat
To know and appreciate,
If you knew the joy that Jesus can give,
You never would hesitate,

To ask for His Spirit, as it says in His Word,
To fill and immerse you with love,
He'll give you such joy, and His wonderful peace
Will come down like a heavenly dove.

*Psalm 34:8 (NKJV)*
*Oh, taste and see that the LORD is good;*
*Blessed is the man who trusts in Him!*

# King at Last

In the middle of the winter,
When everything is dread and drear,
When days are short and nights seem endless,
Sweet robins' song we do not hear.

When grass is dead and covered over,
With a blanket of soft snow;
When all the trees stand tall and naked
And the north winds howl and blow.

It is then we have a season,
Jesus' birth we celebrate;
He came when time was ready;
He never was or will be late.

This time is full of joy and gladness,
There is a spirit of hope and love;
I'm so glad we have a Christmas,
God sent His Son from heaven above.

Soon another day is coming,
The time now approaching fast;
He'll break through the clouds in glory,
A reigning, ruling "King at Last!"

*Zechariah 14:9 (KJV)*
*And the Lord shall be king over all the earth;*
*in that day shall there be one Lord and his name one*

# Precious Promises

So many precious promises
In Your written Word I see,
Help me apply each one, dear Lord,
Because they are for me.

If You were standing here, Lord,
In my living room today,
And I was anxious over cares,
In love I'd hear You say,

"Let not your heart be troubled,
Neither let it be afraid,"
You bore the heavy burden,
The awful price You paid.

You're just the same today, Lord,
As You were so long ago,
So help me be a doer
With these precious truths I know.

**John 14:27 (NKJV)**
*"Peace I leave with you,*
*My peace I give to you;*
*not as the world gives do I give to you.*
*Let not your heart be troubled,*
*neither let it be afraid.*

# Prince of Peace

The future is uncertain; the outlook may be bleak,
The stock market may plummet, the economy has become weak.
Still in your heart you have a song – and you have peace,
If you know Jesus.

The clock will strike the midnight hour;
Will things remain, will we have power?
Still in your heart, in worst of times you will have peace,
If you know Jesus.

The ark will rise above the storm,
Inside the ark you're safe and warm,
Though waves and violent waves increase,
Still in your heart, there's perfect peace,
If you know Jesus.

*John 14:27 (KJV)*
*Peace I leave with you, my peace I give unto you:*
*not as the world giveth, give I unto you.*
*Let not your heart be troubled, neither let it be afraid.*

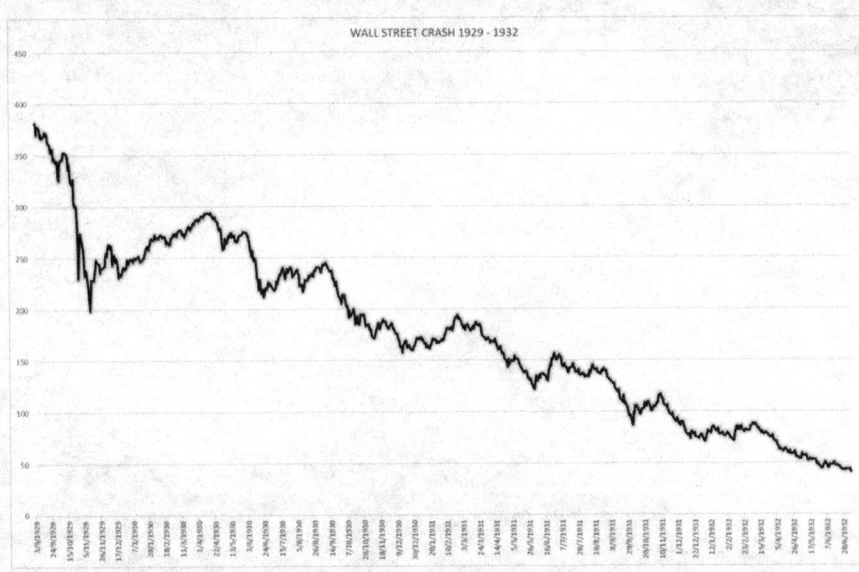

## The Storm

My heart cries out, oh, Jesus,
You're the only One who knows;
How fearful and alone I feel
When the mighty tempest blows.

Your disciples cried, "We perish!"
When they were out to sea.
The same great peace You gave to them,
One night, You gave to me.

You are so wonderful, oh, Lord,
Why should I fearful be?
"Increase my faith!" my prayer would be
On life's uncertain sea.

*Matthew 8:23-26 (KJV)*
*And when he was entered into a ship, his disciples followed him. And, behold, there arose a great tempest in the sea, insomuch that the ship was covered in waves: but he was asleep. And his disciples came to him, and awoke him, saying, Lord, save us: we perish. And he saith unto them, Why are ye fearful, O ye of little faith? Then he arose, and rebuked the winds and the sea; and there was great calm.*

## I Give to Thee

I give to Thee dear Savior,
My every trial here;
My every tribulation,
My every doubt and fear,

When I begin to reason,
From my human point of view,
I begin to sink like Peter,
When I take my eyes off You.

You are the Master Craftsman –
And I a piece of clay.
And as I trust Thee, Jesus,
My burdens roll away.

*Matthew 11:29 (NASB95)*
*Take My yoke upon you
and learn from Me,
for I am gentle and
humble in heart, and
YOU WILL FIND REST
FOR YOUR SOULS.*

## I Have Arrived

I abide, yes, I live in Your presence my Lord,
I remain in Your glorious rest,
What glorious peace, indescribable joy
I'm no longer in search of a quest.

The world passes on, I no longer belong,
I live in an awesome new realm.
I've died to this life and all that it holds
I've taken my hands off the helm.

I live in a state of expectancy,
He shows me glorious things;
With outbursts of joy, my arms raised to the sky
My mouth freely breaks forth and sings,

I've arrived, I've arrived praise God I've arrived!
"Would I leave?" don't bother to ask,
I will stay, I will stay in His glorious rest
I will stay in His Sonlight and bask.

*Psalm 106:1 (NKJV)*
*Praise the LORD!*
*Oh, give thanks to the LORD, for He is good!*
*For His mercy endures forever.*

Composed July 18, 1991

# Deep In His Love

My time everyday
With the Lord, with the Lord,
With yielded heart,
Gather seed from the sword,
The Spirit quickens it
In my heart.
I die to allow the seed to sprout,
My roots go down deep
In His marvelous love.
New life springs forth;
Praise the Father above.

*Ephesians 3:17 (KJV)*
*That Christ may dwell in your hearts by faith;*
*that ye, being rooted and grounded in love.*

# United In Love

Let us go into the presence of Jesus,
Let us go into His courts with praise;
Oh let us exalt His Name together,
In adoration to Him, our voices we raise.

We thank You and praise You oh Heavenly Father,
For answering prayer in a beautiful way;
For leading us on, from glory to glory
And teaching us patiently day after day.

We come from Your throne, lifted higher and higher,
Our hearts overflow in a river of love;
Refreshed and revived, after being with Jesus,
Together we worship, united in love.

*Psalm 100:4 (NKJV)*
*Enter into His gates with thanksgiving, and into His courts with praise.*
*Be thankful to Him, and bless His name.*

# I Will Praise Him

I will praise Him when I'm going through
A valley dark and cold,
When my friends can't seem to help me,
Or I wandered from the fold.

I will praise Him when I find it hard
To read His Word and pray,
When I must wait upon the Lord,
To show me plain the way.

I will praise Him when His endless love,
Comes shining through once more,
Communion is restored with Him
Just like it was before.

He is worthy, He is worthy
To receive all praise from me;
So I'll keep on praising Jesus
'Till His loveliness I see.

*Psalm 18:3 (NASB95)*
*I call upon the LORD, who is worthy to be praised, And I am saved from my enemies.*

Composed December 16, 1999
# Jesus Filled Me

Jesus filled me with the Spirit,
The Spirit made Jesus real to me,
He then drew me to the Father,
Blessed, blessed Trinity.

*Ephesians 5:18 (KJV)*
*And be not drunk with wine, wherein is excess; but be filled with the Spirit.*

Composed September 8, 2007

# Soar

You can soar above your problems,
You can rise above the storm,
For Jesus is your Shepherd
And in His arms you're safe and warm.

Satan cannot touch your spirit,
In Jesus Christ your strength is found,
Let Him be your Great Defender,
And soar above this battle ground.

But you must rest on every promise,
And do not try to understand,
For everything there is a purpose,
Just trust and hold His nail-scarred hand.

When this fiery trial is ended
And once again you laugh and sing,
You'll be as gold refined and stronger,
A precious jewel fit for the King.

**1 Peter 1:18, 19 (NKJV)**
*... you were not redeemed with corruptible things, like silver or gold, but with the
precious blood of Christ, as of a lamb without blemish and without spot.*

Composed August 21, 1990

# Wonderful Jesus

More exciting than –
More magnificent than –
More beautiful than –

For He's more wonderful
Then my mind can conceive,
He's more wonderful
Then my heart can believe,
He goes beyond my highest hopes
And fondest dreams –
He's everything
That my soul ever longed for,
Everything I wanted
And so much more;
He's more than amazing –
More than wonderful –
More than miraculous
Could ever be;
For He's more wonderful –
That's what Jesus is to me.

*John 10:10 (KJV)*
*The thief cometh not, but for to steal, and to kill, and to destroy:*
*I am come that they might have life, and that they might have it more abundantly.*

# CHAPTER 10
# PRAYER

## A Prayer for Mothers

I cleaned my house good last week,
I dusted and washed all the floors,
I polished and waxed and put things away,
Wiped fingermarks off the doors.

I cleaned the shelves and washed the cupboards last week,
Baked rolls and a coffeecake too,
I ironed on patches and sewed up some seams,
Cleaned the woodwork until it looked new.

Today, as I walk through the place
And gaze here in utter dismay,
The dust has returned, the beds and the floors
Are once more in bad disarray.

Sometimes, it seems there will be
No end to this tiresome task
Of being a mother, a housewife and friend,
But Lord there is one thing I ask.

Keep me loving and sweet day by day,
As I serve both my family and Thee,
Help me be kind and forgiving to all,
So that they may see Jesus in me.

I don't want to labor in vain,
Time flies and soon will be past,
Help me do all my work as to Thee,
For I know then, for You it will last.

*Proverbs 31:27 (NKJV)*
*She watches over the ways of her household,*
*And does not eat the bread of idleness.*

## A Summer Day

Some men say that there is no God
But they should come to my house.

The beautiful morning, there are soft rays of sunlight,
Streaming in my front room window.
A soft, balmy breeze floats in, allowing me to enjoy
The first sweet scents of summer.
Birds are singing merrily in the trees and each one
Has a different melody.

*Psalm 14:1 (KJV)*
*The fool has said in his heart, "There is no God."*

Composed November 8, 2002

## Becoming One

My arms are open wide.
Come, like a child, run fast to Me.
With great excitement,
Jump off the highest cliff of trust and know that I will catch you.
Do not be afraid,
Search for Me with all your heart,
Search and you will find Me.
Walk deep into the forest of faith.
Do not be afraid.
Jump into the deep waters of My love,
Let My love overwhelm you.
Be filled and swim in My love.
Stay close to Me.
Die to self.
Totally surrender and
Become one with Me.

*Luke 6:46 (KJV)*
*And why call me, Lord, Lord and do not the things which I say?*

Composed November 5, 2009

# Endure

You're almost there,
You're goin' up the rough side of the mountain now,
But keep climbin' child, keep climbin',
You're almost at the summit,
Don't, don't look back, just keep climbin'.
It won't be long, you're gonna' see the King;
Think of it!
The King in all of His glory!
Imagine the first glimpse of Him,
"The King of Kings"
Keep laborin' on, no one said it would be easy.
As soon as you arrive,
You'll forget all of your pain and heartache,
Whatever you do, don't give up now!
Lean hard on Him,
Just a little bit further and you'll reach the peak.
His love is drawing you;
His love is giving you strength,
He's taking you from glory to glory –
Hallelujah! Hallelujah!
You're becoming desperate for Him now,
You've never known a love like this,
You've never imagined a love like this,
His love is strong, it will bring you home.
Endure, Endure,
"Endure to the end."

Philippians 4:13 (NASB95)
*I can do all things*
*through Him*
*who strengthens me.*

Composed March 19, 1993

# From the Quiet Place

In these very quiet, flat times,
When I do not sense Your strong presence in my life,
I realize, yes, I know very well
That it is not me at all in the overflowing times,
When there is that gushing forth from deep within.

That overflow did not originate from my mind,
Nor from my emotions, as some may have supposed.

Lord, I know, how I very well know
That I am but a cold, empty clay vessel,
Just waiting to be filled and used.

I wait for You to turn the water into wine again my Lord.

*Isaiah 40:31 (KJV)*
*But they that wait upon the Lord shall renew their strength.*

Composed November 8, 1993

# Hear the Voice of the Father

Come, please come, oh be very still my child.
Come face to face with Jesus every day.
Look long and deep into His blessed eyes.

There you will see agape love, mercy, tenderness,
Kindness, peace, long suffering, gentleness,
Purity, goodness and tears.
At last, you will see eternity.

His eyes reveal what is in His heart for you.
He is yearning to flood you with what is in His heart.
Only then can you go out and face the giants in the land,
For only His perfect love will cast out all fear.

*Psalm 68:19 (NASB95)*
*Blessed be the Lord, who daily bears our burdens.*

# In Him We Live

Know Me,
Be intimate with Me,
For your complete total well-being,
Obey Me.

In every circumstance you find yourself,
In every situation you face,
In all your dealings with men,
Women and children today,
Obey Me.

Do the thing I would do,
Say the thing I would say,
Act in a way I would act.

For when you obey Me,
All of My power,
All of My grace,
And all of My authority is behind you.

What a beautiful, satisfying and joy-filled day
You will experience as you walk
In the obedience of Christ Jesus.
And when the day comes to an end,
There will be no regrets.

*Galatians 2:20 (KJV)*
*I am crucified with Christ: nevertheless I live; yet not I, but Christ liveth in me:*
*and the life which I now live in the flesh I live by the faith of the Son of God,*
*who loved me, and gave himself for me.*

Composed June 14, 2005

# Look to Me

Do not look to this day as though it were a mountain
Or to the week ahead as though it is a very heavy load,
Look to Me.
I am with you every step of the way.
I will give you strength.
Tell fear to go.
Do not be overwhelmed by anyone or anything but Me.
Abide in Me.
Rejoice!
Enjoy this day!

*Isaiah 49:13 (KJV)*
*Sing, O heavens; and be joyful, O earth; and break forth into singing, O mountains:*
*for the Lord hath comforted his people, and will have mercy upon his afflicted.*

Composed December 2011

# One Star

On that night so long ago,
One bright star guided the wise men
To the manger.

In this present darkness,
There is only one star,
Jesus,
"The Bright and Morning Star."

*John 8:12 (KJV)*
*I am the light of the world; he that follows me shall not walk in darkness,*
*but shall have the light of life.*

Composed February 28, 1993

# No Words

Sometimes we are overwhelmed in grief, there are no words.

At times we are overwhelmed with happiness once again,
there are no words.

Many things we experience, we find there are just no words
to adequately describe what we are going through.

What I am experiencing goes beyond any human experience.
It is without a doubt, absolutely impossible to describe,
because it is in my spirit.

It goes beyond, beyond mere words. The love, the love I have for you.
How very warm it makes me Lord, to know that this love is mutual,
You love me too.

*Isaiah 41:10 (KJV)*
*Fear thou not; for I am with thee:*
*be not dismayed; for I am thy God:*
*I will strengthen thee; yea, I will help thee;*
*yea, I will uphold thee with the*
*right hand of my righteousness.*

Composed August 1, 2003

# Strands and Chords

With strands of love,
He knit me together in my mother's womb.

Through life
The strands often become twisted and tangled.

Sometimes they unravel.
I must go back to the Knitter,

He is compassionate,
He is here in my suffering,
His tears mingle with mine.

With strong chords of love,
He begins to mend and repair me.

I am fortified,
I am strengthened,
I am stronger than I was before.

I can go on.
I believe I can soar.

*Psalm 139:13 (NASB95)*
*For You formed my inward parts;*
*You wove me in my mother's womb.*

Composed January 10, 2003

## Sacrifice of Worship

There is an altar within my soul
Where a sacrifice of worship and praise
Is being offered up to God my Father
For giving His Son for me.

Being drawn deeper into His love,
That I see, is far greater than the universe
Is causing my heart to break forth and erupt.

In the beauty of holiness,
I am "knowing" love,
In the truest, purest sense of the word.

In this most divine place
That I have ever been,
That I ever knew was possible,
There is a constant flow of tears-
At last, I believe, enough to wash His feet.

*Psalm 96:9 (KJV)*
*O worship the Lord in the beauty of holiness: fear before him, all the earth.*

Composed October 3, 2005

## To Soar

To soar,
Our roots must go deep
Into the soil of God's marvelous love.

Our depth determines our height.

*Ephesians 3:17 (KJV)*
*That Christ may dwell in your hearts by faith;*
*that ye, being rooted and grounded in love...*

# The Greatest Gift

The greatest gift that you can give,
To friends and family while you live;
It really shows how much you care,
If you spend time for them in prayer.

A lovely gift tied with a bow,
Conveys your love, it lets them know,
But gifts will surely pass away,
It's better still to kneel and pray.

Some carry loads beyond belief;
The broken homes, the pain, the grief;
We need to love, we need to share
The burdens that so many bear.

Some suffer pain and some despair,
They need to know that others care;
For when you say, "I'll pray for you,"
Your words bring hope and strength anew.

*Ephesians 6:18 (KJV)*
*With all prayer and petition pray at all times in the Spirit,*
*and with this in view, be on the alert with all perseverance*
*and petition for all the saints.*

# There is a Balm

There is peace, there is joy.

Be immersed,
Drink deeply from the streams of living water.
As you drink,
The waters will sweetly and gently
Wash away the pain and hurt.

I trust You in this midnight hour,
I lean on You and trust Your power,
You are my source, I live in You.
Entwined with God in all I do.

*John 15:5 (NASB95)*
*I am the vine, you are the branches; he who abides in Me and I in him, he bears*
*much fruit, for apart from Me you can do nothing."*

# Your King

Come bride of the Lamb,
You who desire Him only,
Come with the cymbal and dance,
Come and worship Him.

Bow down before Him,
Holy, Holy, Holy
Is His name,
Come with your vestures.

Dipped in blood,
For He has purchased you.
Oh, worship, worship, worship
Your Redeemer, your Savior, your King.

*Revelation 19:13 (NASB95)*
*He is clothed with a robe dipped in blood, and His name is called The Word of God.*

**CHAPTER 11**

# SALVATION

## All

He paid a very great price to save us,
He took the punishment for our sin.
The sin of every person on earth was upon Him,
He wanted our hearts to win.

He said, "Follow Me," and He walked to the cross;
The gift of salvation is free.
But to follow Him, we must give Him our all;
For His cost was death on a tree.

This is not religion, God ponders our heart;
He will say to many, "Depart!"
We must guard our eyes and ears,
And love Him with all our heart.

We must turn from worldly attractions,
We must walk the long narrow way.
We must love Him with all of our heart and soul;
Jesus said, "I am the way."

*Matthew 22:37 (KJV)*
*Jesus said unto him, thou shalt love the Lord thy God with all thy heart,*
*and with all thy soul, and with all thy mind.*

Composed December 2008

# Believe

The beautiful story of Bethlehem
Is not just an age-old fable.
God really did send His Son;
He was born inside that stable.

But greater still than Bethlehem,
Is a place called Calvary,
Where Jesus Christ laid down His life
And was crucified for me.

We simply cannot conceive,
But we're not told to understand,
We simply must "Believe!"

*Acts 16:31 (KJV)*
*And they said, "Believe on the Lord Jesus Christ,*
*and thou shalt be saved, and thy house."*

# Choose Jesus

Corruption is sweeping the nation;
There's strife and unrest everywhere,
But you can have peace like a river,
Just knowing that Jesus is there.

There's pleasure in sin for a season,
But what can compare with the joy
That He gives when we follow Him fully,
His power we can fully employ.

Trust Jesus, He'll take you to heaven
And daily He'll walk by your side;
The Holy Spirit bears witness
And He will forever abide.

*Matthew 11:28 (NASB95)*
*Come to Me, all who are weary and heavy-laden, and I will give you rest.*

# Come

I just cannot tell you
And it's grieving my heart,
I am just not able
To begin to impart.

This life in the Spirit
That He's given to me,
It is beyond comprehension
And beyond degree.

You've got to go to the river
And you've got to drink;
Don't try to understand it all,
It's not what you think.

Seek God with your whole heart,
Let Him be your guide;
Jesus bids you to come
To the other side.

*2 Corinthians 6:2 (NKJV)*
*For He says:*
*"In an acceptable time I have heard you,*
*and in the day of salvation I have helped you."*
*Behold, now is the accepted time;*
*behold, now is the day of salvation.*

# Drink

Drink deep from the wells of salvation,
You will find these waters are sweet,
Drink 'til you drown out his lying,
When he screams in your ear "defeat."

*Isaiah 12:3 (KJV)*
*With joy you will draw water from the wells of salvation*

September 18, 1998.

# Follow Me

After You fed the hungry,
After You healed the lame,
They turned on You and shouted –
"You are the One to blame!"

After the wedding in Cana,
You made wine for one and all,
When You cried "I Thirst" they gave You
Vinegar and gall.

After You laid Your hands on a man
Causing his eyes to see,
They pierced Your hands and feet with nails
While spilling out blasphemy.

After seeing the bitter rejection
That began in Gethsemane,
I shrink back and hide in the shadows,
When you say, "Come, follow Me."

Will I walk the long difficult road
Or take the broad easy road,
You have said "I will never leave you,
I will help you carry the load."

If you lose your life you will find it,
Forsake it all and be free,
I know the path you must travel,
Let Me guide you, "Follow Me."

*Matthew 5:44 (NKJV)*
*But I say unto you, love your enemies,*
*bless them that curse you,*
*do good to them that hate you,*
*and pray for them*
*which despitefully use you,*
*and persecute you.*

Composed August 24, 2003

# Frosty White

All alone in the darkness,
I knew I was not saved,
I was sent up to my bedroom
Because I had misbehaved.

The Holy Spirit convicted me
And I began to cry,
What if Jesus would come back?
What if I should die?

I tried so hard to go to sleep,
But sleep I could not find,
I knew I was a sinner,
And that I'd be left behind.

Should I call down to my parents?
I had been so very bad,
I had no choice, I must get saved,
I called down to my dad.

Together, kneeling down by the couch,
In a precious holy glow,
My father led me to the Lord
That night so long ago.

I prayed a simple prayer,
The words came from my heart,
Jesus died for all my sins,
Believing was my part.

I was not in a great cathedral,
That cold mid-winter night,
But as I wiped away the tears I saw
The panes were frosty white.

*Romans 10:13 (NKJV)*
*For "whoever calls on the name of the LORD shall be saved."*

Composed June 19, 2002

## The Paradox

The more you die,
The more you'll live;
A paradox indeed,
But we would be
So very wise
If this message
We would heed.

If you love your life,
You'll lose it,
And you will abide alone.
God's word is true,
You can expect
To reap what
You have sown.

*Galatians 6:8 (KJV)*
*"For he that seweth to his flesh shall of the flesh reap corruption;*
*but he that seweth to the Spirit shall of the Spirit reap life everlasting."*

# Intercede

There's evil lurking in the streets
And crime is on the rise;
Old Satan's going to and fro,
To fill our mind with lies.

Most people don't know where to turn,
Their hearts are filled with fear;
Some even sense that judgement
Is drawing very near.

Precious souls are in the balance,
So few Christians seem to care;
We're all so very busy or
Don't see the need for prayer.

God paid a price to save us,
He saw our dire need;
Should we not have compassion
And take time to intercede?

*Hebrews 7:25 (NKJV)*
*Therefore, He is able also to save forever those*
*who draw near to God through Him,*
*since He always lives to make intercession for them.*

# Receive His Gift

Down through the ages God saw you,
He had to find a way
To bring you back to Himself;
You were lost, so far astray.

Trying to fill the void in your life
You never did succeed.
Only Jesus could go deep enough
To meet your deepest need.

He would take away that emptiness
He would set your spirit free
He would give you a rich abundant life
Now and eternally.

God knew the gift you needed most,
For you He sacrificed
His only Son on Calvary's cross
Jesus paid the awful price.

If we neglect or plain refuse
This gift straight from God's heart
There is no more God can do
Except to say, "Depart."

If we believe He died for us
We must give our heart, our life
God freely will impart to us
His gift, "Eternal Life."

This gift for us is priceless
It will never pass away,
Above, beyond all other gifts
Receive His gift today.

OUGHT AND PAID FOR

*Romans 6:23 (NKJV)*
*For the wages of sin is death;*
*but the gift of God is eternal life*
*through Jesus Christ our Lord.*

Composed December 11, 2004

# Seek Jesus

Why are you so unhappy,
You seem to have all you need.
You're crying for living water,
You need on Jesus to feed.

Seek Jesus

Do not stop 'til you find Him,
He's the One for whom your heart aches,
He, your Creator, the Giver of Life –
Seek Jesus, He patiently waits.

*Matthew 6:33 (KJV)*
*But seek ye first the kingdom of God, and his righteousness;*
*and all these things shall be added unto you.*

# The Great Commission

Everywhere, everywhere, there are people in need;
People in bondage who cry to be freed.
Many are lonely with minds filled with fear,
They need to know that the Savior is near.

He longs to give them His wonderful peace;
For only in Him can they find full release.
He would forgive all their guilt and their sin,
And His own Spirit would flow from within.

May we who know Jesus as Savior and Friend,
Continue His work with a heart that will lend,
For we have the secret to set the world free,
The great commission is for you and for me.

*Matthew 28:18-20 (NKJV)*
*And Jesus came and spoke unto them, saying, all power is given unto me*
*in heaven and in earth. Go therefore, and teach all nations, baptizing them*
*in the name of the Father, and the Son, and the Holy Ghost:*
*Teaching them to observe all things whatsoever I have commanded you;*
*and, lo, I am with you always, even unto the end of the world. Amen.*

Composed July 12, 2001

# The Leper

"Unclean, unclean!" I cried, "Unclean!"
I was full of leprosy.
"Stay away, stay away,
Don't come too near
Or you will become like me."

Alone, alone, I was so alone,
People passed and shook their head,
No one could heal my putrid sores,
I laid helpless on a bed.

Afraid, afraid, I was so afraid,
Filled with pain and haunting fear,
The longing for a loving touch,
But no one could come near.

But He came, He came, He came to me-
And He stood so very near!
He tenderly reached out His hand,
And He cast out every fear.

He touched me and He healed me,
Then He said, "Come, follow Me,
I will give you rich abundant life
Now and eternally."

*Leviticus 13:45 (NKJV)*
*Now the leper on whom the sore is, his clothes shall be torn and his head bare;*
*and he shall cover his mustache, and cry, 'Unclean! Unclean!'*

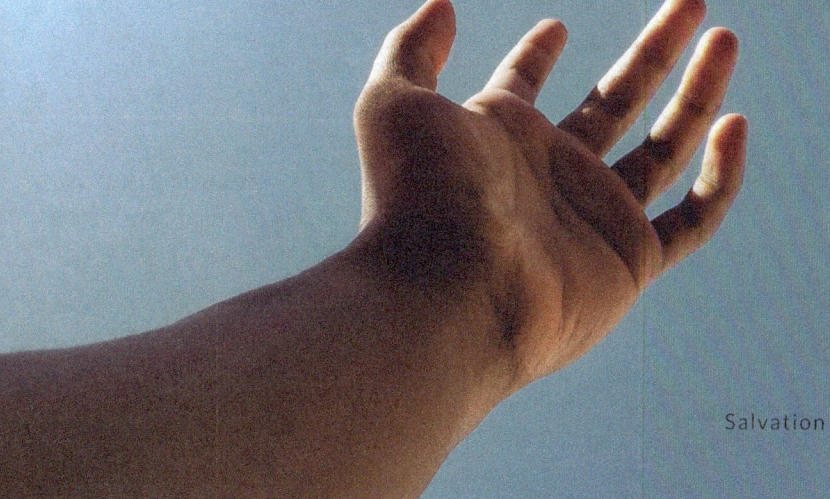

# CHAPTER 12

# THANKFULNESS

## Thanksgiving Day

Give Thanks
For God's bountiful table,
His Word
We must "Taste and See."

We may eat at any time from His table,
It is fresh,
It gives strength,
It is free.

*Psalm 34:8 (NASB95)*
*O taste and see that the LORD is good;*
*How blessed is the man who takes refuge in Him!*

# This Day

I want to take
A few minutes today,
To say thank you Lord,
For this beautiful day.

For the beautiful shade
Of blue in the sky
And the lovely white clouds
As they slowly drift by.

For all of the birds
Making sweet melody,
It seems like today
They're singing for me.

For the soft, gentle cooing
Of a beautiful dove;
Which reminds me again
And again of Your love.

For the wonderful fragrance
Just filling the air,
Your love in creation
Is seen everywhere.

He's created these things
For you and for me;
But we take them for granted
Because they are free.

*Colossians 1:16 (NKJV)*
*For by Him all things were created, both in the heavens and on earth,*
*visible and invisible, whether thrones or dominions or rulers or authorities—*
*all things have been created through Him and for Him.*

# Sunshine

For the lovely morning sunlight,
For each hazy shimmering ray,
That softly says, "I love you-
I'll be with you through this day."

For the brilliant noon day sunlight,
As it shines high in the sky;
Bringing life to field and forest,
Without the sunshine, we would die.

For the beauty of a sunset,
Radiant gold, low in the west;
For welcomed peaceful darkness,
Again, allowing us to rest.
Thank you, Lord

*Psalm 113:3 (NASB95)*
*From the rising of the sun to its setting,*
*The name of the LORD is to be praised.*

# TRUSTING

Composed March 17, 2004

## Drinking

Drinking deeper, deeper from the living waters,
Stretching for the things that lie before,
Trusting, trusting Jesus as my Savior,
Yearning deeply still to know Him more.

Forsaking everything but Christ my Savior,
Gaining, pressing forward for the prize,
Going on from glory to glory,
As an eagle, soaring higher in the skies.

*Psalm 112:7 (NASB95)*
*He will not fear evil tidings;*
*His heart is steadfast,*
*trusting in the LORD.*

## Just Flow

Like a beautiful river
That flows through the land,
Flow in the Spirit
As He holds your hand.

Trust Him completely
Throughout every day,
Not by might nor by power
He alone knows the way.

*Zechariah 4:6 (KJV)*
*Then he answered and spoke unto me saying,*
*this is the word of the Lord unto Zerubbabel,*
*saying, not by might, nor by power, but by my spirit, saith the Lord of hosts.*

## God Loves You

What shocking news we heard today –
A loved one you must lay away,
What can we say, what can we do,
Except to say that God loves you.

His Son asked "Why?" when on the cross,
God turned His back, oh what a loss.
You too ask "Why?" but trust Him still,
And with His love, your hearts He'll fill.

Oh trust God through this bitter hour,
Lean hard on Him and His power,
And through these days what e'er you do,
Trust God and know He still loves you.

*Psalm 62:8 (NKJV)*
*Trust in Him at all times, you people;*
*Pour out your heart before Him;*
*God is a refuge for us.*

Composed December 14, 1998

# Mold Shape

Trusting the hand of the Potter,
I am His, I am the one of His fold
Even if He wants to start over
I will yield to the shape of the mold.

**Isaiah 64:8 (KJV)**
*But now, O LORD, thou art our father;*
*we are the clay, and thou our potter;*
*and we all are the work of thy hand.*

Composed August 10, 2005

# Salvation and Discipleship Cost

I am famished, I am hungry,
I'm longing for the deeper life,
I want the food that He only offers,
I need Him, The Bread of Life.

It is not by simply gazing
At the cross where Jesus died,
I must also walk to Calvary,
And like Him be crucified.

To be His true disciple,
To bear more of His fruit,
I must lose my life to find it,
Follow Him in hot pursuit.

Only Jesus can go deep enough
To meet my deepest need,
"This is the way, walk in it"
I must follow where He leads.

The price is high and very costly,
To follow Jesus Christ my Lord,
My eyes, my heart are fixed upon Him,
Jesus is my great reward.

*Matthew 16:24 (NKJV)*
*Then said Jesus unto his disciples,*
*"If any man will come after me, let him deny himself,*
*and take up his cross, and follow me."*

Composed September 29, 2005

# Trusting You

It is by simply trusting
This is the path for me,
All other paths are stressful
Full of complexity.

I must stay on this path Lord,
Holding tightly to Your hand,
Trusting You with all my heart
When I do not understand.

*Proverbs 3:5-6 (KJV)*
*Trust in the Lord with all thine heart;*
*and lean not unto thine own understanding.*
*In all thy ways acknowledge him, and he shall direct thy paths.*

Composed December 18, 1997

## Divine Revelation

I cannot worship You in my mind, oh Lord
I cannot begin to start,
I must have Your impartation,
Holy Spirit move my heart.

The depths, the depths, the depths of Your Love,
Like a rose bud with its beauty concealed,
Is opening up in the depths of my soul,
My God, You are being revealed.

*John 4:24 (NKJV)*

*"God is Spirit, and those who worship Him must worship in spirit and truth,"*

Composed October 12, 2007

## Baptism of Love

Consumed with Jesus in my being,
He grows sweeter every day,
Moved at times with deep compassion,
Constrained by love, to care, to pray.

Abundant life for God descending,
Dying now to self and pride,
Finding His divine fulfillment
In my soul for which He died.

No clouds between, just sweet communion,
With my Father up above.
Immersed and filled and running over,
He baptized me in Calvary love.

*Matthew 3:11 (NASB95)*

*As for me, I baptize you with water for repentance, but He who is coming after me is mightier than I, and I am not fit to remove His sandals; He will baptize you with the Holy Spirit and fire.*

# The Waters

I want to take you to the waters
Where the grass is rich and green;
It is a very special place,
Very special and serene.

We meet there in the morning,
His sweetness permeates the air,
He wraps His arms around me,
Fills me with His Spirit there.

I love You, oh I love You Lord,
How glorious when we meet,
There is no place I'd rather be
Then here Lord, at Your feet.

*1 Chronicles 16:29 (NKJV)*
*Give to the LORD the glory due His name; Bring an offering,*
*and come before Him. Oh, worship the LORD in the beauty of holiness!*

# God My Father

Oh Lord, my God Your holiness,
Your majestic power and might,
Made known within my spirit
In the very dead of night.

So unworthy, in Your presence,
In awesome silence I adore,
Holy, holy glory,
Now and evermore.

May I come; do I still call You Father?
In great love He reaches to me.
"Keep your eyes on the cross,
Precious child, I am God, I am Love, I am He."

*Psalm 99:5 (NKJV)*
*Exalt the LORD our God, and worship at His footstool – He is holy.*

Composed March 8, 1991

# Lift My Soul

My soul lifts up its voice and cries,
You are the Lord,
You are the Lord.

I crucify my flesh and find,
It slowly dies,
It slowly dies.

Oh Lord Your glorious life comes forth,
Your life in me,
Your life in me.

Abundant life so rich and free
You give to me,
You give to me.

Soon I will hear the trumpet sound
Then quickly rise,
Then quickly rise.

To be with You forever Lord,
Beyond the skies
Beyond the skies.

*Psalm 46:1 (KJV)*
*God is our refuge and strength.*

# Draw Near

Draw nearer to Me,
Draw nearer to Me,
When things all around
Would terrify thee,
Don't look without,
For I am within,
Be calm and be still;
Draw nearer to Me.

*James 4:8 (KJV)*
*Draw nigh to God, and he will draw nigh to you.*
*Cleanse your hands, ye sinners; and purify your hearts, ye double minded.*

Composed February 28, 1999

# Worship in Winter

It is winter, God,
I am dead and full of winter,
But I will praise You
Even though my heart is hard and cold.

You gave for me
The darling of Your bosom,
You would have given Him
For me alone.

As I worship You,
The barrenness of winter,
Begins to leave my soul,
My heart can sing.

I sink into the depths
Of love surpassing,
And know again
The hope and thrill of spring.

*Psalm 22:3 (KJV)*
*But thou art holy, O thou that inhabitest the praises of Israel.*

# Acknowledgments

I want to thank my nephew, Allen Slager, Sr., for encouraging me with the development of *Feeding in His Pasture*. Together, we had spoken about publishing the poems and writings I had written, over many years. We had been praying and asking God to send a publisher our way. The Lord moved in a mighty way. Alan Mostert has been a friend of my nephew, for over 50 years. Alan Mostert was in the publishing business, with his brother. Growing up, my nephew and Alan Mostert had been involved together in church activities. Outside of church, they would participate in sports during their teenage years. Our prayers had been answered for a publisher.

Also, to my grandson, Nicholas, who has been a pure joy to me throughout my life. He would run from his school bus to have a snack with me. We had such quality time together. It is my desire, that he pursue Christ, becoming the man that God has called him to be.

I want to thank everyone who has encouraged me to publish my poems and writings. Throughout the years, many friends who have read my writings have told me to share these with others. I thank them so much.

To the rest of my family, I thank them for being there for me throughout this season of my life. I also acknowledge my family of friends from Open Bible Christian Center in Kankakee, Illinois.

It is my prayer that *Feeding in His Pasture*, will bless every reader, for the glory of God. May our Lord Jesus Christ, use *Feeding in His Pasture*, to encourage, comfort and teach the glorious truths from His Word.

> *Now unto Him that is able to keep you from falling,*
> *and to present you faultless before the presence of His glory*
> *with exceeding joy, to the only wise God our Savior, be glory*
> *and majesty, dominion and power, both now and ever. Amen.*
> Jude 1:24, 25 (KJV)

In Christ,

*Audrey Hill*

# Index of Poems

# E

# F

# G

# H

# I

# Index of Scriptures

# Index of Categories

# Photo Credits

96   Summer lake; Photo by Bill Howell

97   Photo by Denys Nevozhai-Duo, Unsplash

98   Photo by Sulthan Auliya, Unsplash

100  Camp entrance 1 Timothy 1:15 sign; Photo by Bill Howell

101  One drop poem; Open Eye_Dropper_-_The_Noun_Project.jpeg.

102  Photo by Phil Hearing, Unsplash

104  Large logs; Photo by Bill Howell

106  Clouds above trees; Photo by Bill Howell

109  Swirling water; Photo by Bill Howell

110  Photo by Yoal Desurmont, Unsplash

109  Armor of God; Internet Archive Book Images, No restrictions, via Wikimedia Commons

114  Evening light; Photo by Bill Howell

114  Photo by Daniel Salcius, Unsplash

116  Photo by Mott Rodeheaver, Unsplash

117  Salt shaker; Photo by Trey Schatzmann, Unsplash

118  Story Book Lodge chapel pulpit; Photo by Bill Howell

119  Freestocks, Unsplash

121  Heart; Photo by Ed Robertson, Unsplash

122  Blue winter sky; Photo by Bill Howell

123  Photo by Dorsa Fathollahi, Unsplash

124  Footwashing; Public domain, via Wikimedia Commons

125  Photo by Shraga Kopstein, Unsplash

129  Photo by Zwaddi, Unsplash

130  Loaves and fishes; Photo by Brotvermehrungskirche_BW_3-2 1.7mb

132  Photo by Christina Rumpf, Unsplash

133  Photo by Engin Akyurt, Unsplash

134  Apples; Photo by Bhawnagusain174, CC BY-SA 4.0 <https://creativecommons.org/licenses/
     by-sa/4.0>, via Wikimedia Commons

136  Decorative wall and brick; Photo by Bill Howell

139  Sunrise; Photo by Charley9, CC BY-SA 3.0 <https://creativecommons.org/licenses/by-sa/3.0>,
     via Wikimedia Commons

142  Prepared food; Photo by Ms Jones from California, USA, CC BY 2.0 <https://creativecommons.
     org/licenses/by/2.0>, via Wikimedia Commons

144  Bride; Photo by outreachr.com, CC BY 2.0 <https://creativecommons.org/licenses/by/2.0>, via
     Wikimedia Commons

146  Tile floor; Photo by Bill Howell

149  River between hills; Photo by Bill Howell

150  Lion; Photo by Iván Díaz on Unsplash

153  Photo by Sixteen-Miles-Out, Unsplash

154  Falling stock chart; Photo by Encik Tekateki, CC BY-SA 4.0 <https://creativecommons.org/
     licenses/by-sa/4.0>, via Wikimedia Commons

156  Brick fireplace; Photo by Bill Howell

159  Photo by Rishabh Pammi, Unsplash

161  Evening moving sky; Photo by Bill Howell

163  Photo by Isaac Maffeis, Unsplash

167  Photo by Benaja Germann, Unsplash

168  Photo by Kate Mclean, Unsplash

172  Camp entrance sign; Photo by Bill Howell

177  Frosty window panes; Public domain, via Wikimedia Commons

181  Photo by Pixls.am, Unsplash

182  Table settings; Photo by Bill Howell

184  Photo by Jordan Steranka, Unsplash

185  Water flow; Photo by Bill Howell

189  Photo by Alexander Milo, Unsplash

192  Photo by Dominik Schroder, Unsplash

187  Potter's wheel; Photo by Wknight94 talk, CC BY-SA 3.0 <https://creativecommons.org/licenses/
     by-sa/3.0>, via Wikimedia Commons

190  Clouds rolling; Photo by Bill Howell

# About the Author
## AUDREY HILL

Audrey Hill was born in the heart of the winter, in January 1941, during the height of World War II. She was raised in the Roseland neighborhood, on the South Side of Chicago, Illinois. She is the fourth child of her parents, Henry and Alice Muys. Her parents were faithful followers of the Lord Jesus Christ. The younger years of Audrey Hill were influenced by her parents' godly living and teaching. Through their guidance, it was instilled in her to live an honoring and glorifying life for God.

Her humble upbringing and hard life experiences, endured in her early years of loss and disappointment, did not cause her to detour, or waver, from developing a deep love and faith in the Lord Jesus Christ. She always exemplified a genuine love of family and friends over her lifetime.

She speaks of her love for her savior Jesus, as she recalls the night she gave her life and heart to Him. She was a young, nine year girl. To this day, Audrey Hill is a totally committed and devoted follower of the Lord Jesus Christ.

After her marriage to Ron Hill in 1961, she left Roseland and moved to Harvey, Illinois. After living there for a short period of time, they were able to move 40 miles south, to a farm in rural Bourbonnais, Illinois. As they settled in to country living, they were able to adopt two children, Ronda and Nathan.

After her husband's passing, she lived independently for many years, until she went to live in an assisted living center.

She has walked through many peaks and valleys throughout her life and God has always been there for her. God has been faithful through many trials, troubles and tests, which gave Audrey Hill a solid insight into scripture. Throughout the years of living on the farm, her roots started to grow deeper and deeper into God's marvelous love. Audrey Hills's poetical genius and Biblical knowledge, is seen in the poems and prayers she has written in *Feeding in His Pasture*.

Audrey Hill has a passion to see lost souls won for Christ. One of her greatest desires is to see multitudes come to faith in Jesus Christ. Through her writings, she also seeks to encourage believers in Christ, to grow in the grace and knowledge of our Lord Jesus Christ. These are the items which were the inspiration for *Feeding in His Pasture*. Audrey Hill hopes many will benefit from reading it and be changed for the glory of God.

Life has been full and rich for her. It is her prayer, that *Feeding in His Pasture* will encourage the reader to seek out Jesus and to stay faithful to God and His word. Giving all praise, honor and glory to our great God and savior Jesus Christ.

Made in the USA
Monee, IL
22 July 2025

21684547R00115